Journeys: Iceland
Don Hodell Chilcote

Foreword:

Tales from the unquenchable spirit for learning the path through the garden of discovery over the triumph of the land. This book is a memento of hope for todays world and its hurting people. Many people will relate to the intensity of human spirit to discover the beauty in this world and travel to the ends of the earth. People these days want the instant entertainment and the spectacle of life. I have invented my own trail and discovered, toiled and failed. I was never interested in the becoming unbreakable and starkly perfect. I am more interested in shattering with grace and courage those journeys that strengthen my soul and making art of it all the broken pieces. My hats off to all the original souls like 80s rock artists with one offs on a Casey Casum hit list. Souls who get back up more times than they are knocked down, and who give more than they ever expect to receive. These are tales of those who smile and show love through the sad times and the support the victims of bullied absurd spirits. Tales of travel for inspiration to find the beauty in this concrete jungle of madness. Honor is given to those who light the way for others and who spread laughter and joy. Celebrate the uniqueness of each and every soul not made from a boxed cereal clone. We thank those who build humanity and make the world a better place, and share stories of courage and tired legs. We lift up those who do something unique in this world that impacts. We soar to give a soul the courage to dream to define legacy.

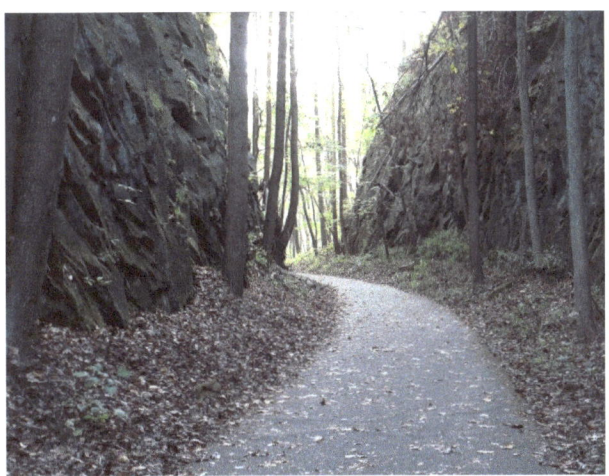
Black Hand Gorge, Ohio

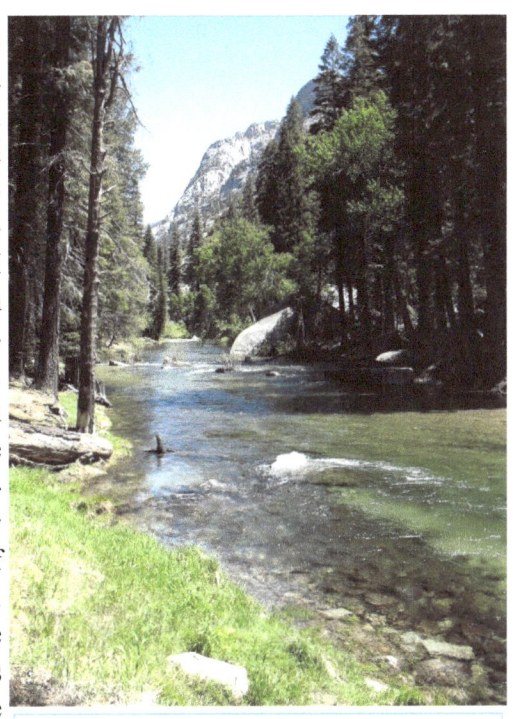
Kings Canyon, California

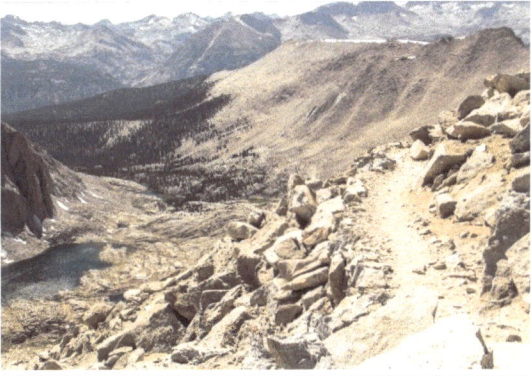
Mount Whitney Trail, California

So step over ants and get your hands dirty and put worms back in the grass and rescue baby caterpillars. Release those spiders back into your garden before squashing them, and open windows for bees to fly home. Stop fertilizing your mansion before insects all disappear as they are all little souls that deserve a life too. So take vacations not to sit on a beach but to revel in the newness of the journey. Go as many places as you can and realize that you can always make money, but you cant always make memories. If you ever fail remember it means first attempt in learning. I've been stuck in the quicksand and off the trail for miles. It is the journey that defines you, and not someone else's framing in their limited viewpoint. Remember in the end that effort never dies and if you get no as an answer it means next opportunity.

Treat everyone with attention they deserve. The goal of life is to give and not become a celebrity. Live in a way that makes everyone around us feel celebrated. Challenge the one who has to hear themselves talk all the time and command the floor. Remember to live beneath your means and return everything you borrow and stop blaming other people for your own shortcomings. Admit it when you make a mistake and do something nice and try not to get caught in the politics of crap. Listen more and talk less and everyday take a walk to renew your mind. Strive for excellence and not perfection and be on time and don't make excuses and don't argue. Get organized, and be kind to all peoples including those with amazingly sour souls. Brighten others hearts, take time to be alone, to dream always, and cultivate good manners and respect. Be humble and realize and accept that life isn't fair and know when to keep your mouth shut. You got to know when to hold them, know when to fold them, know when to walk away, and know when to run. Learn from the past and plan for the future and live in the present. Don't sweat the small stuff and its all small stuff in the end. No matter what the only thing that matters in what you have given the world and its people. This is so much more important than the wining and dining and fluff of life. Do not confined by this world but transformed by the renewing of you mind and spirit. Cherish inspiration, creativity, and inspiration paying it forward to others always.

I was born in San Francisco, California and grew up Cleveland Heights, Ohio. The community was a fairly diverse. I attended a local Presbyterian church, grew up in Roxboro grade school, and went to University School. I also have degrees from the University Of Rochester, and the Ohio State University. My first journeys were at the waterfall place in South Chagrin metropark in Cleveland, Ohio and on the property of the Nature Center, chasing crickets in the hills of Chautauqua, Panama Rocks, and Mentor Headlands. The greatest of my early journey were at camp Wabun in Lake Temagemi in Ontario.

The stories in this book are for the most part unscripted journeys to seek out something unique. The poems and songs are a part of the journey as a lot of the ideas were formed from the freedom of the journey. This document was primarily dictated while biking or hiking into an Iphone and arises from the inspiration of the beauty of discovery. Encourage, Travel, Share.

The passion for discovery is infectious. The optimism about any situation is your attitude about being bright shiny and positive about any circumstance and appreciative of the newness of the journey. It transforms you, it renews you, it shapes you, it challenges you, and most of all it gets you back to adventure, and a chance to daydream and be yourself.

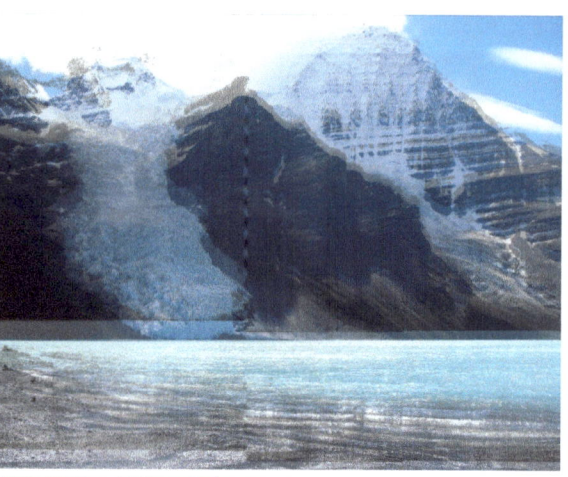
Berg Lake, Alberta, Canada

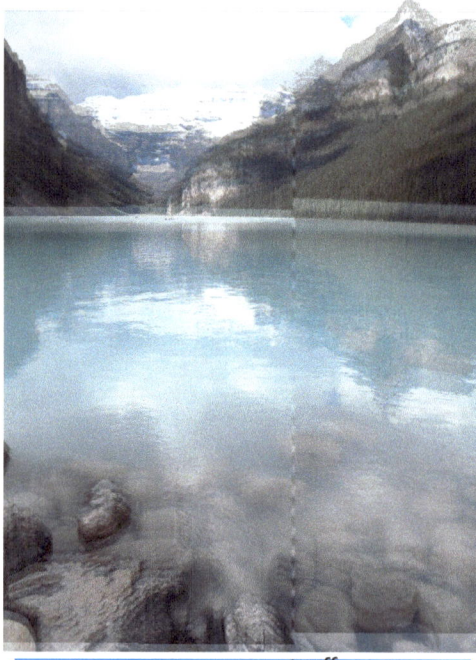
Lake Louise, Banff

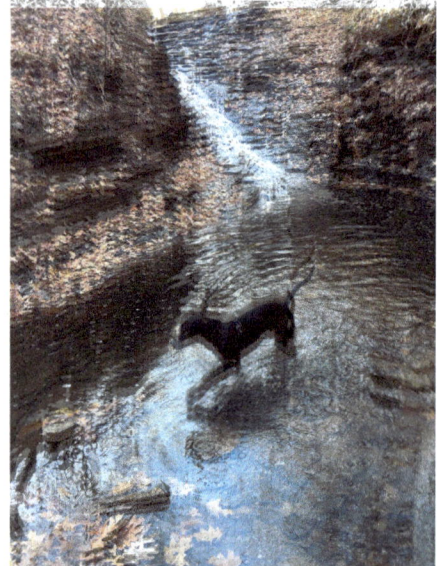
Awesome Dawson in North Chagrin

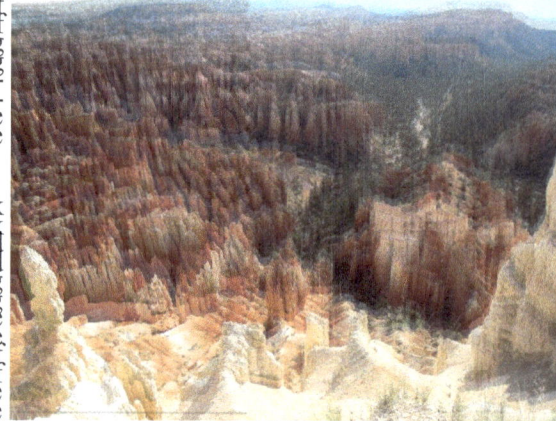
Bryce Canyon, Utah

Journeys: Iceland
Don Hodell Chilcote

Don Hodell Chilcote is a musician living in Cleveland, Ohio. He spends most of his time as a music educator, church pianist, and published composer of all kinds of music. He completed a Masters in Music Composition from Ohio State University as well as BA from the University Of Rochester. Many of his compositions and recordings are published on Sheetmusicplus, Amazon, Itunes, and Cdbaby. In his free time he is an avid explorer as written and illustrated in this travelogue and book. He is described as an curious outdoor adventurer enjoying the journey to the unique. The goal is to actively chase places unknown and photograph all the experiences before either they disappear, become common, or just plain destroyed from overuse. As an educator, he is a person with a servant's heart, giving to teaching of students, elevating worship, and pursuing artist endeavors. The quest, the discovery, the journey into the great untraveled are the inspirations behind this book:

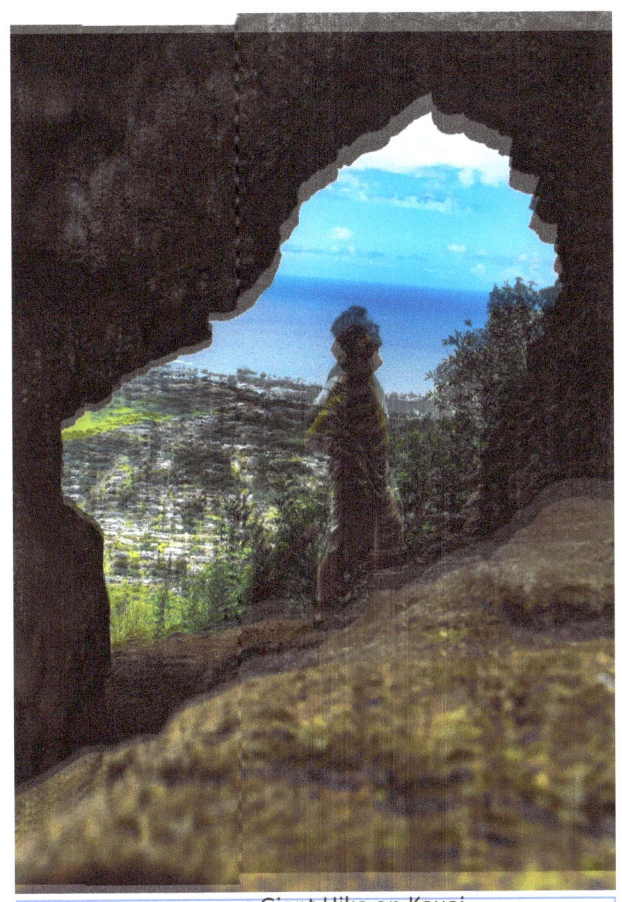

Sleeping Giant Hike on Kauai

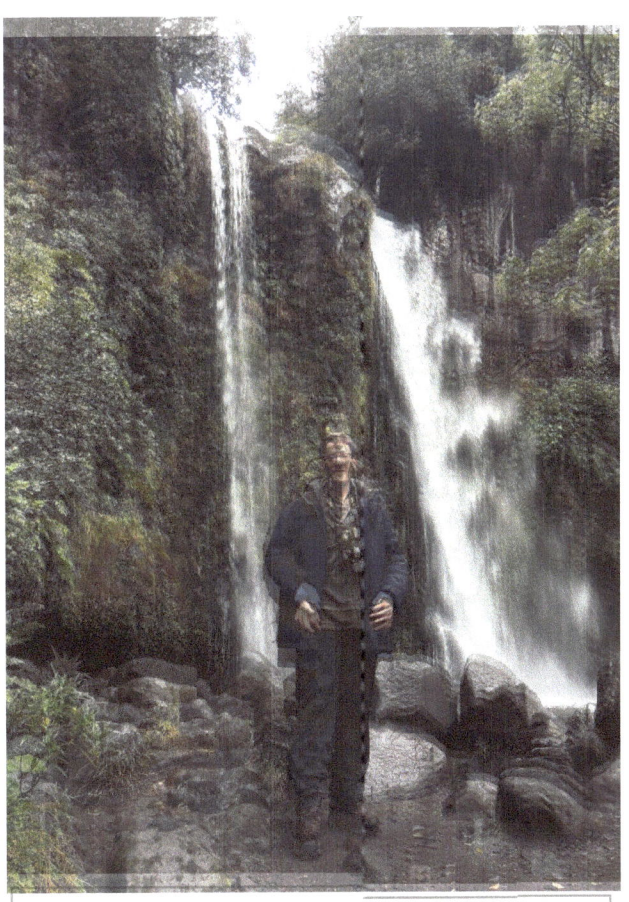

Author at Dawson Falls without Dawson

Table Of Contents

Foreword	Page 1
Poems and Essays:	Page 5-14
Journey:	Page 15-30
Fearlessness	Page 46
Gratitude	Page 49
From Heart To Heart	Page 50
Body and Soul	Page 51
Ending Inspirations	Page 52

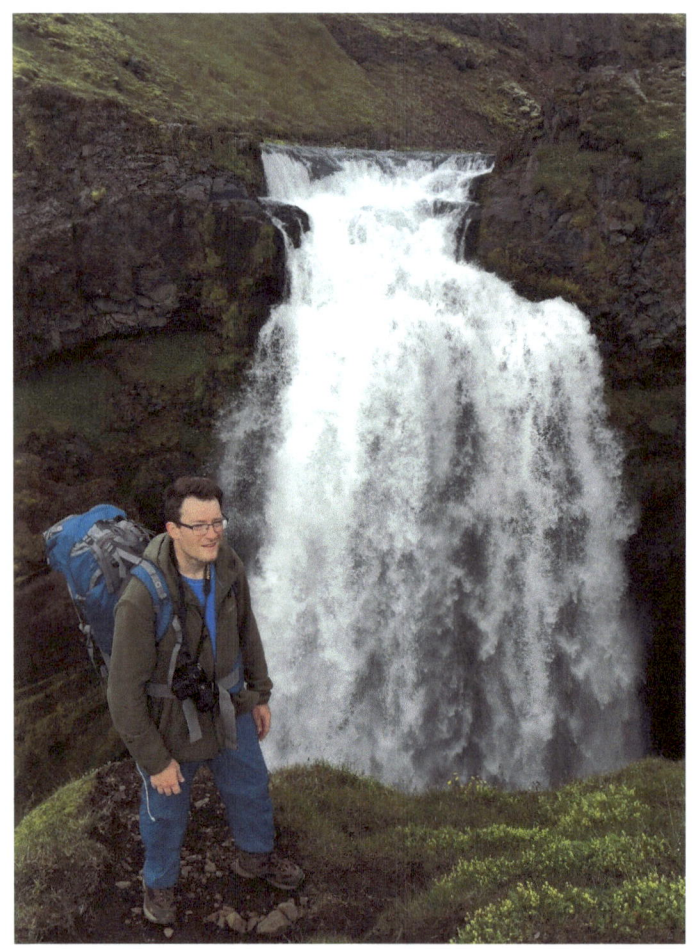

Skogar Trail

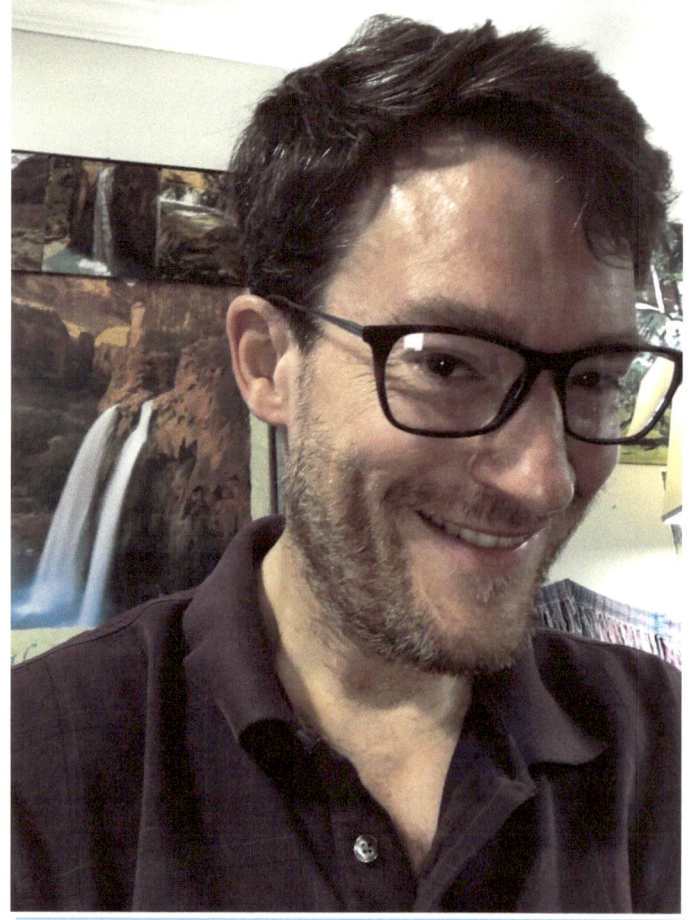

Author with calmness and joy the morning after returning from Traveling in Iceland

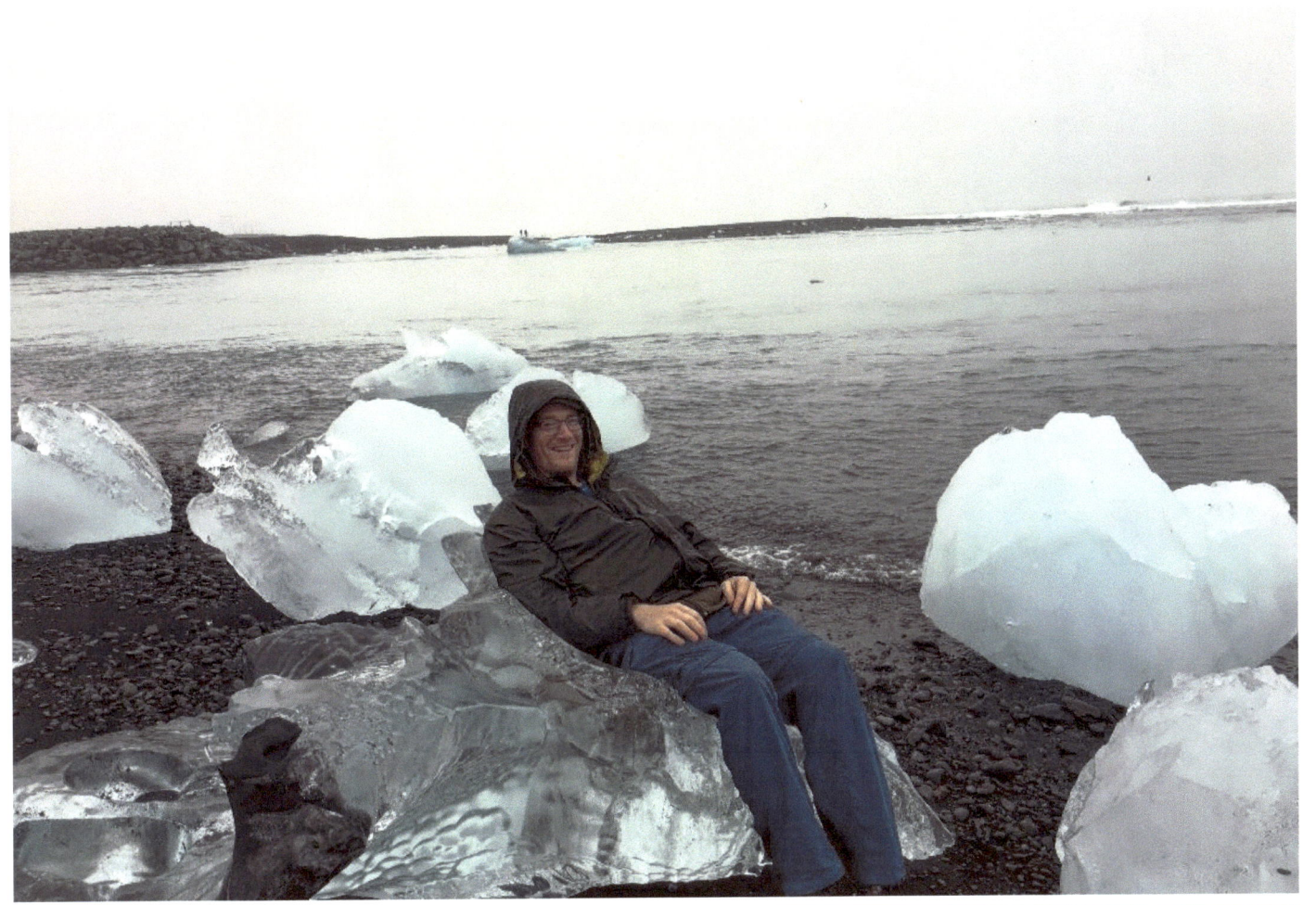

Seriously Cold Ice Chair

Prayer

May your life song sing of God's amazing grace. May your feet be firm and steady in this race, and when the world reflects your image through a mirrored façade, may you always see your beauty through the perfect eyes of God. When your arms are empty, may your heart be full, and the mountains that you face seem possible. When the ground is dry, I pray that you'd have rain, and when the music starts to vanish, you would sing on through your any pain. And when God's voice is silent, you'd hold tighter to his hand, and trust he'll lead you safely, on the journey he has planned. When threadbare faith holds stillborn dreams, I pray any hurt would be redeemed. So hold on tightly to the Savior, grow in truth, and never waiver. I pray your heart is warm when life can be so cold, and when hecklers and scoffers mock your journey, you'd be bold. I pray for food on your table in times when it's lean; And that you'd share your meal with others, so God's goodness can be seen. This I pray: That you'd have God's best.
Be strong and blessed.

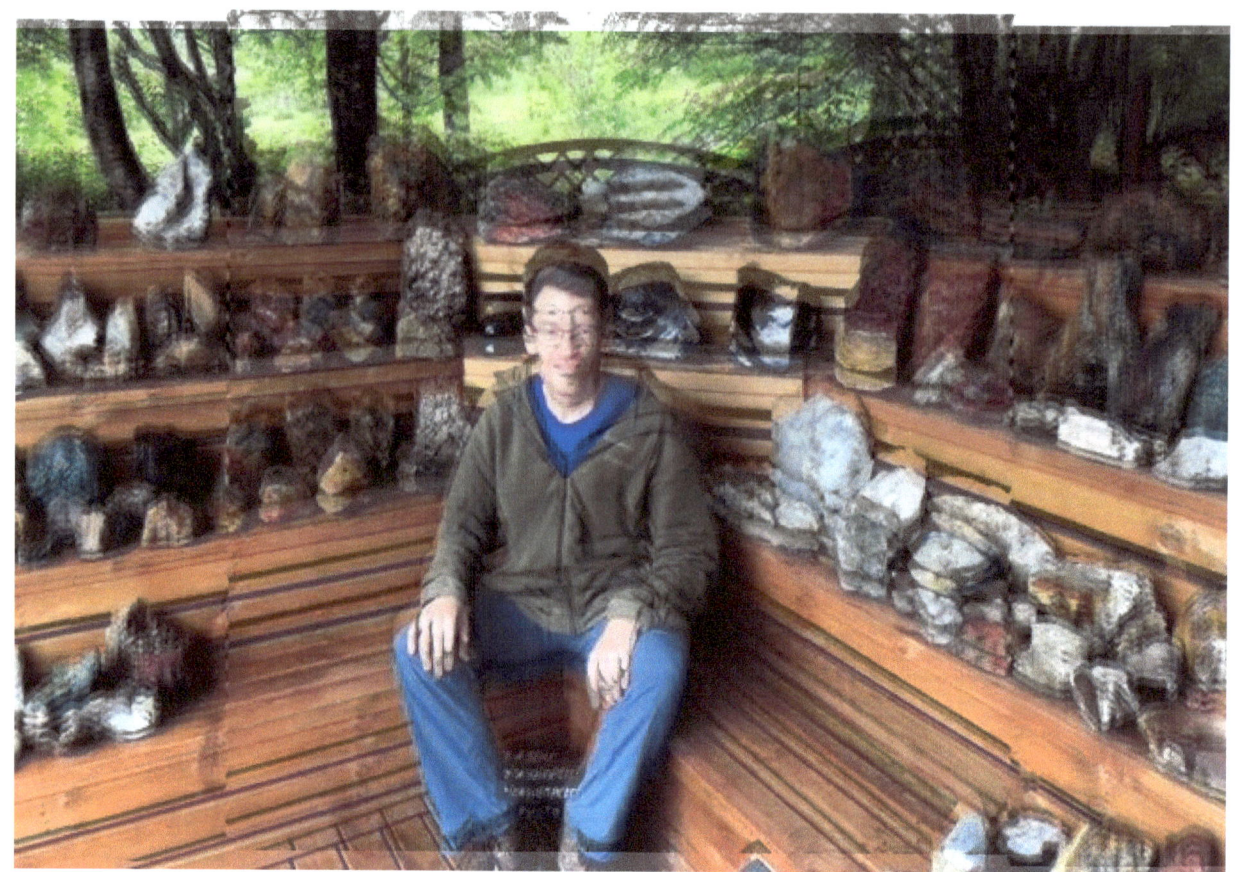

Petra's Stones

Open Doors

Every day is an opportunity to be kind to yourself. Tomorrow is a new opportunity to reset and refocus, and every day is an opportunity to be the person you want and are meant to be. Never forget that when one door closes, another one opens. There are always challenges, disappointments, and setbacks. That's life! But how you respond is 100% in your control. Search for the opportunity to learn, grow, and change. Today's setback can make you stronger and wiser and more appreciative of the life ahead. The elephant keeps walking as the dogs keep barking. When the world seems to be barking at you, staying grounded in your beliefs, and that makes it possible to tune out the noise. To remain true to what you know is right and good is giving yourself a tremendous gift. Every thought, word, and action that you take must pass the three gatekeepers of life: Is it kind? Is it necessary? Is it true? This is worth repeating: Kind. Necessary. True. When you are faced with a choice, makes it an act of positive power. People first. Then money. Then things. Problems? Find the humor, blow up the paradox, and adopt the change. At the end of the day, it really is this simple. Relationships are always your first priority. Never let anything get in the way of nurturing your relationships. Including taking care of yourself, with rest being so very important. Only when you are taking care of yourself will you have the strength and heart to give to others. Sometimes, our yesterdays present irreparable things to us; it is true that we have lost opportunities which will never return, but God can transform this destructive anxiety into a constructive thoughtfulness for the future. Let the past sleep, but let it sleep on the bosom of Christ. Leave the irreparable past in his hands, and step out into the irresistible future with him.

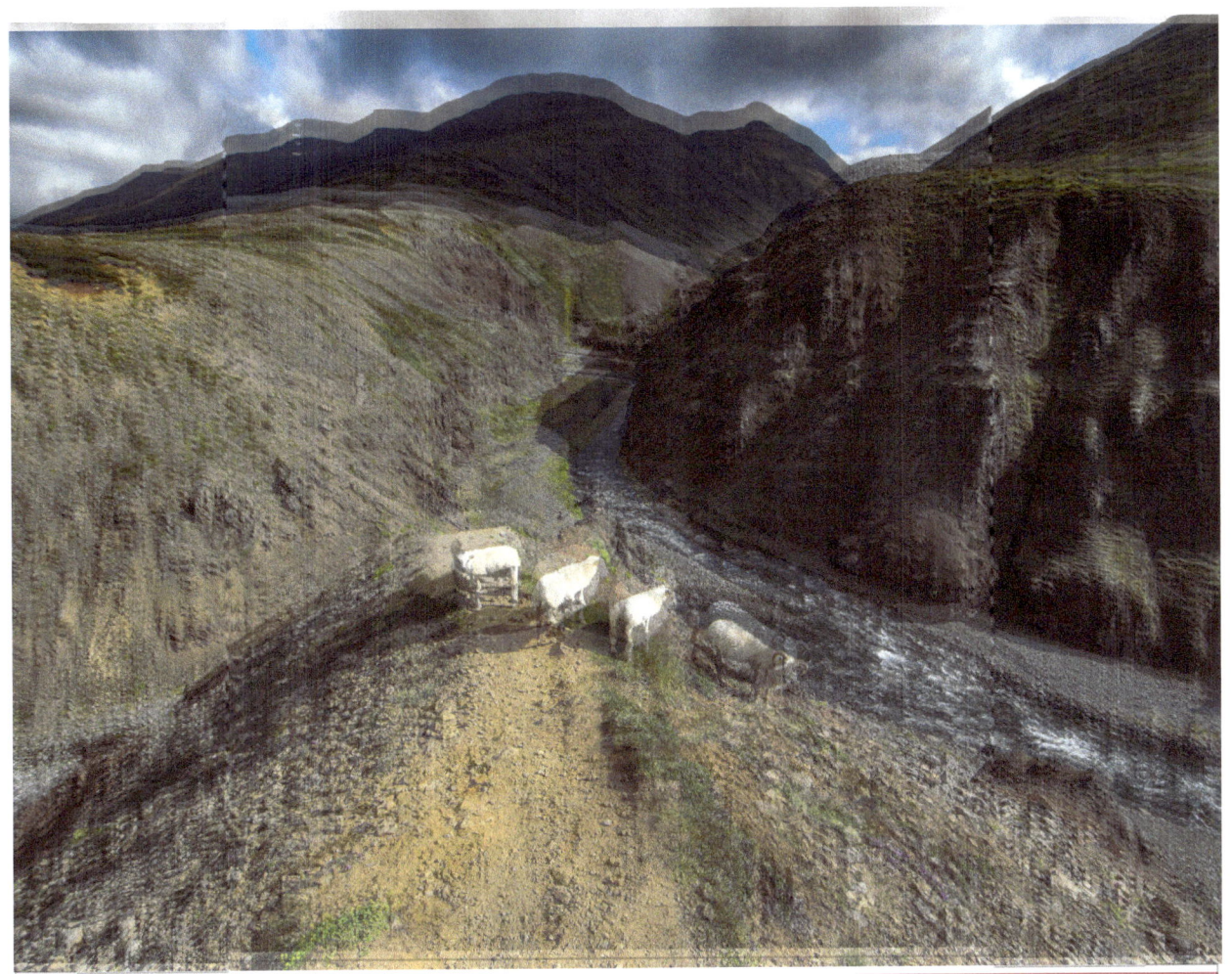

Stand off with Goats

The End Game

It's not about who broke your heart, it's about who mended it. It's not about the times you put your self esteem in the hands of others. But instead, the days where you knew your worth. It's not about those who let you down, but rather those who always held you up. It's not about the many people who desired you. It's about the ones that value you. In the end it's not about all the times you were called beautiful, it's about all the days you felt you were, and the beauty you impacted, and the ones who make you really feel like you are. Shine on my brother and play your own harp. Don't play what the public wants. You play what you want, and let the public pick up on what you're doing, even if it does take many forever years. Do a combination of the tried and true and trusty and the damp and stale and musty and joyful always. Why steal other joy, and find something to make fun of in your reflection when you can find uniqueness and distinctiveness in some observations and comments, stay in the things that brightens others days.

Fallen Hero

Fallen hero there's no gas in the mast, and I got to make it all last, fallen hero absolute zero, there's no gas in the mast. I got to make the wind to last, heckled in comic banter, and in irregular stride, when you're at your pits, and you've met your squasher of creativity, he'll pick you up. Seeing the cosmic hugh you'll find a new view, he'll pick you up. Love the lord with all your heart, your mind, your soul, all you need is love. Unconditional love for community and people, a passion for curiosity and excellence, love of God and honor for family, learn from imperfections, humility and forgiveness. Stop and stoop to help others. Finish the race, and help others walk humbly with God, turn negatives to positive. Soft spoken, never rough and tumble, chip away at rough exterior, never showed weakness, journey and keep others strong and encourage one another, community, lift up your brother, live in the light, purpose for everyone, and be still my soul. These winds will never last, this storm is sure to pass, this trial is just a test so, I shall not, I shall not, oh, I shall not be moved.

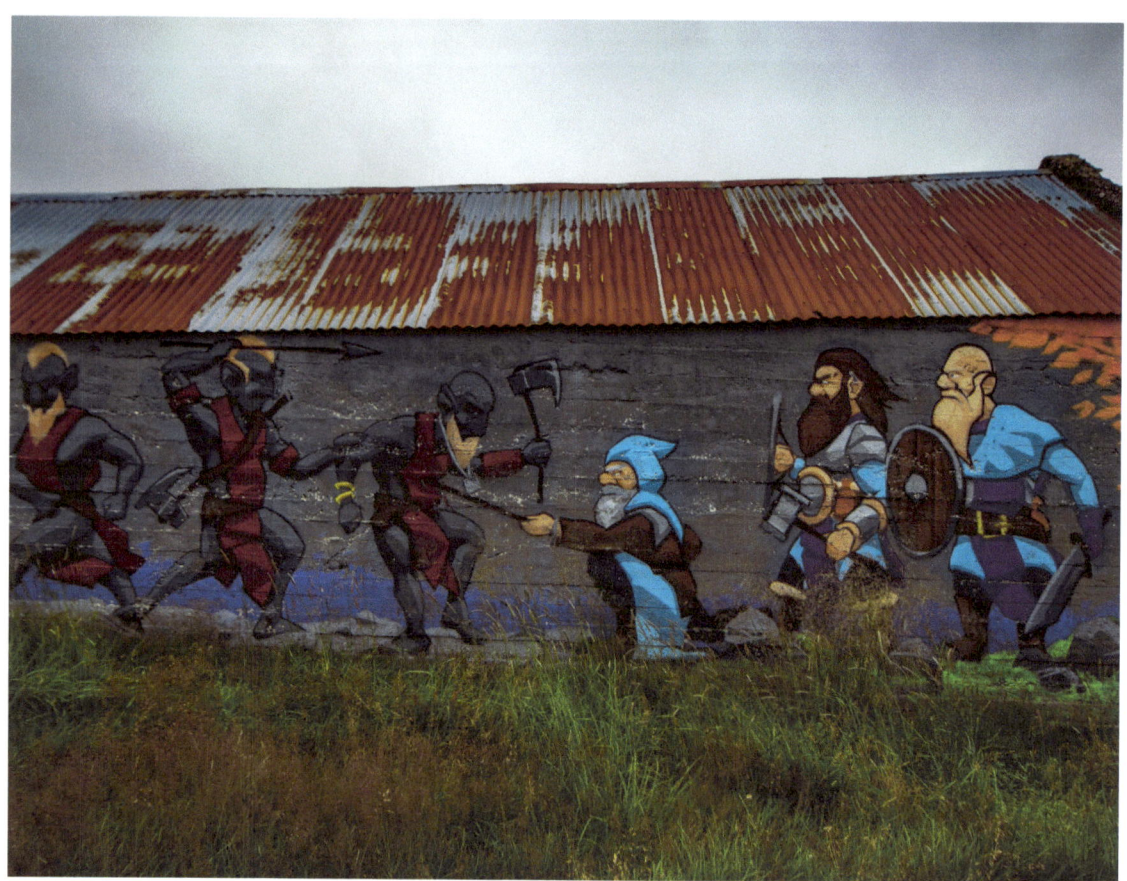

A mural depicting a very important battle

The Threads Of Life

What threads are you made of and what ship do you sail, is it one of compassion for helping what ails. Are you stuck in the privilege, chewing on the cabbage of cardboard, the trailing's or iron ore, and chewing on a belittling spirit. What have you done for the least person in you life, what have you witnessed and supported in all the worlds strife. Why have you not thought of the blessings of creativity, and the blessings of discovery, instead of the escapism and spectacle of the ills of life. No borders can contain my ingenuity, good thoughts and good deeds good ways, and a childlike faith in all. What threads are you made of, what ship do you sail, Is it one of compassion for helping what ails.

Autistic

I am in here, you can't reach me, but I hear you, I want to respond, you can't see it, reach it, but I need you. I'm giving you a stare, but really I am saying I love you, I'm breaking out, I'm moving on, but I'm repeating your intentions. I can teach you to overcome the burn out, and the increased stimulus of the day. You know my kid brother Asperger's. I'm already know that people have sensory oversensitivity which creates anxiety, I filter it daily, and sometimes I'm raw and unfiltered. Pray for me my viewer that I may be, manage, evolve, and win the race for the fight in the battle of the people in the evolving disease, and darkness shall not win.

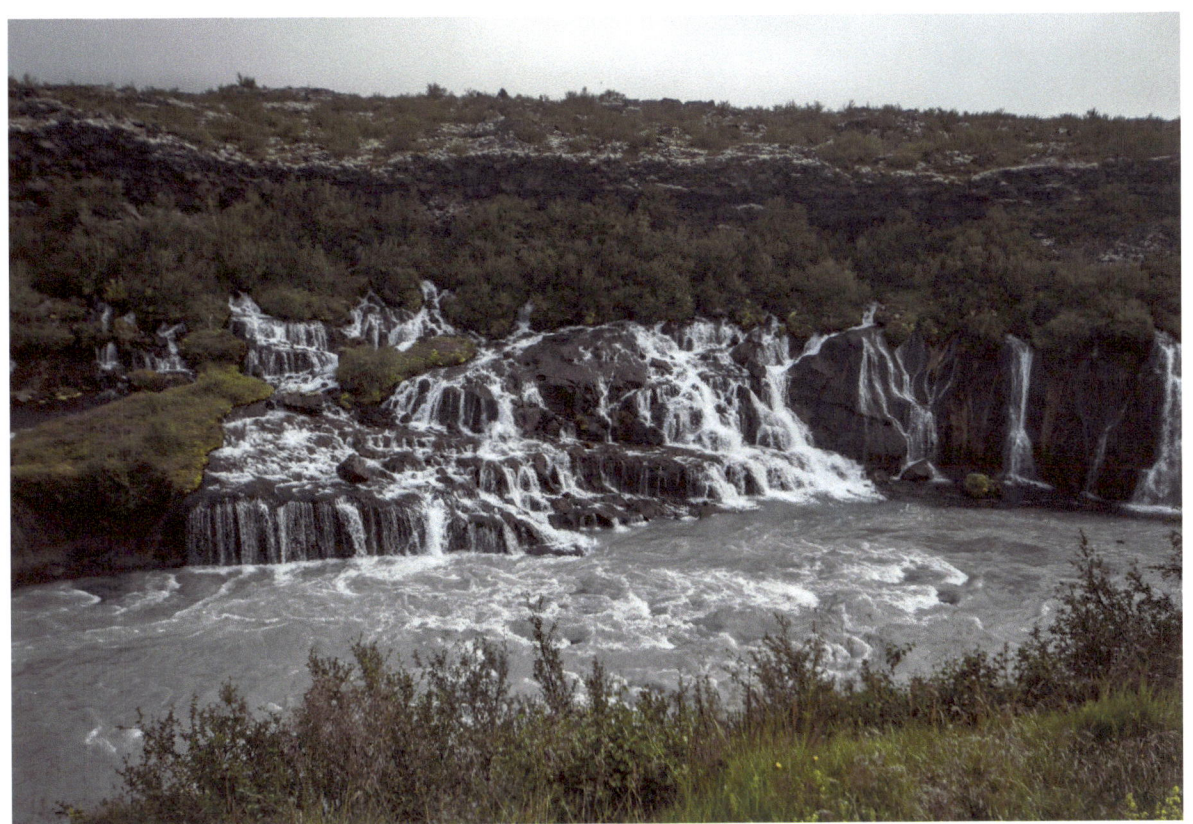

Endless Falls of Barnafoss and Hraunfoss

The Greatest Need

The person with greatest need has least power, the person with greatest power has least need, God has and will supply all our needs, we don't need anything in this world as we have Christ our savior, we always need to live the greatest treasure of all which is to be ourselves and let our little light shine, to live our greatest day in the beauty of the unselfishness and the gorgeous resonating hallway of gratitude. Chip away at those in power but do nothing for the least of these, we have politicians like this. Marvel at the souls who have the action for the compassion. Blessed are you who bear the light. Forgiveness clears the cobwebs, and out of your minds, they get on my last nerve, blessed are you who bear the light in unbearable times, and who testify to its endurance amid the unendurable, and who bear witness to its persistence when everything seems in shadow and grief. Blessed are you in whom the light lives, in whom the brightness blazes, your heart a chapel, an altar where in the deepest night can be seen the fire that shines forth in you in unaccountable faith in stubborn hope in love that illumines every broken thing it finds. Seeing disparity in this world, and not do something about it is a sin, to see opportunity and know where you fit in, and where you lie, your deeds are your monuments, put time into things that matter, pay it forward, not things that tatter, always a heart full of grace, a soul full of gratitude, find those in need and support, and give until you drop.

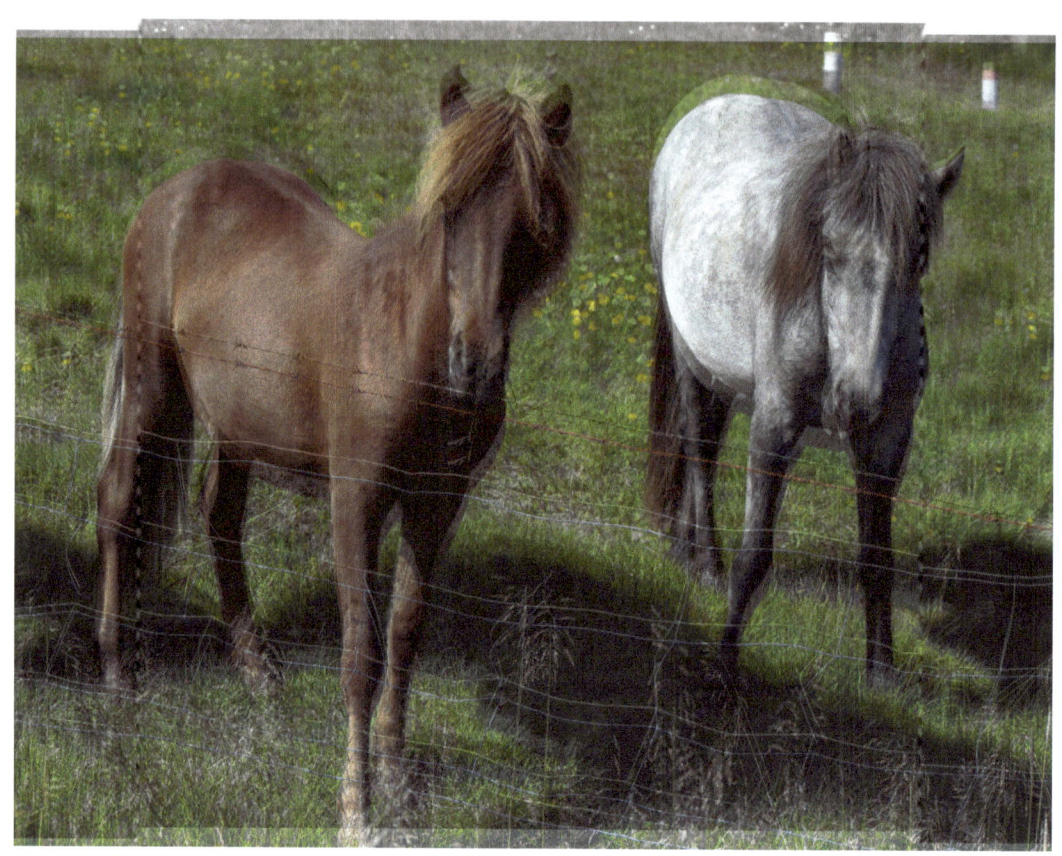

Beautiful Icelandic Horses

The Toughest Things

The tough things in life are like starring into a glassy lake, reflections in the way always, all the answers you are looking for, are there at the bottom, but in between you and them, is the reflection, refraction, and the fog. With maturity you earn the always love mentality, listen and stay close to hear the voice of God, apply the word to your life, ask the lord for an answer, grow in the word, and breathe in prayer, and give thanks daily. The power of spiritual hygiene and the ability to admit wrongness and confess sins. No judging, love on each other with tolerate mindfulness, and a forgiving heart. The best in me, a saviors gift, It's all about love, check yourself before, you wreck yourself. No bitterness, and no judgment. If you live to work all your life then fine, but at least enjoy the journey. Figure out how to work, live, and redefine yourself when you don't work as much and figure out how to live with exceeding great joy at all times. Do not seek happiness. Instead, learn to be content, and happiness will find you. A reasonable man adapts to the world around him. An unreasonable man expects the world to adapt to him. Therefore, all progress is made by unreasonable men, stay true to your vision, but can you please be kind. Are there stolen items from your life, review and obtain them and recapture your vision, love, joy. He who learns must suffer but why, and even in our sleep, there is pain that can not be forgotten, and it must mend drop by drop on the heart. We are only limited by the boundaries of our mind and size of our dreams, and never limited by the naysayer. Be prepared for opportunities, be stretched and constantly challenged, never complacent, and never held back from your potential.

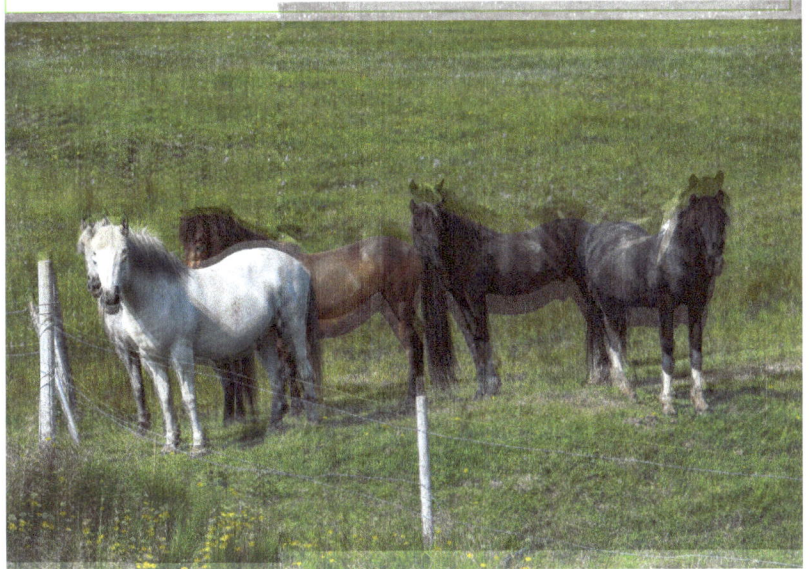

Beautiful Icelandic Horses

Beautiful Icelandic Horses

Misfits And Black Sheep

When your down but not out, simply mistreated but not defeated, there is on thing that brings you back; it is the blessings of gratitude. When you've seen enough favoritism that it becomes mysticism, you just can't understand why more sharing isn't going on maybe lack of caring. Selfishness is on the loose, and it's got a cousin named, I'm done caring about you. Think of the people you've helped. Think the ways of being kept, don't follow the ways of the black crow. Ask the all knowing to order your steps, and be your destiny and your purpose and just be yourself.

Our Greatest Fear

It is our light not our darkness that most frightens us. Our deepest fear is not that we are inadequate. Our deepest fear is that we are powerful beyond measure. It is our light not our darkness that most frightens us. We ask ourselves, who am I to be brilliant, gorgeous, talented and fabulous? Actually, who are you not to be? You are a child of God. Your playing small does not serve the world. There's nothing enlightened about shrinking so that other people won't feel insecure around you. We were born to make manifest the glory of God that is within us. It's not just in some of us; it's in everyone. And as we let our own light shine, we unconsciously give other people permission to do the same. As we are liberated from our own fear, Our presence automatically liberates others.

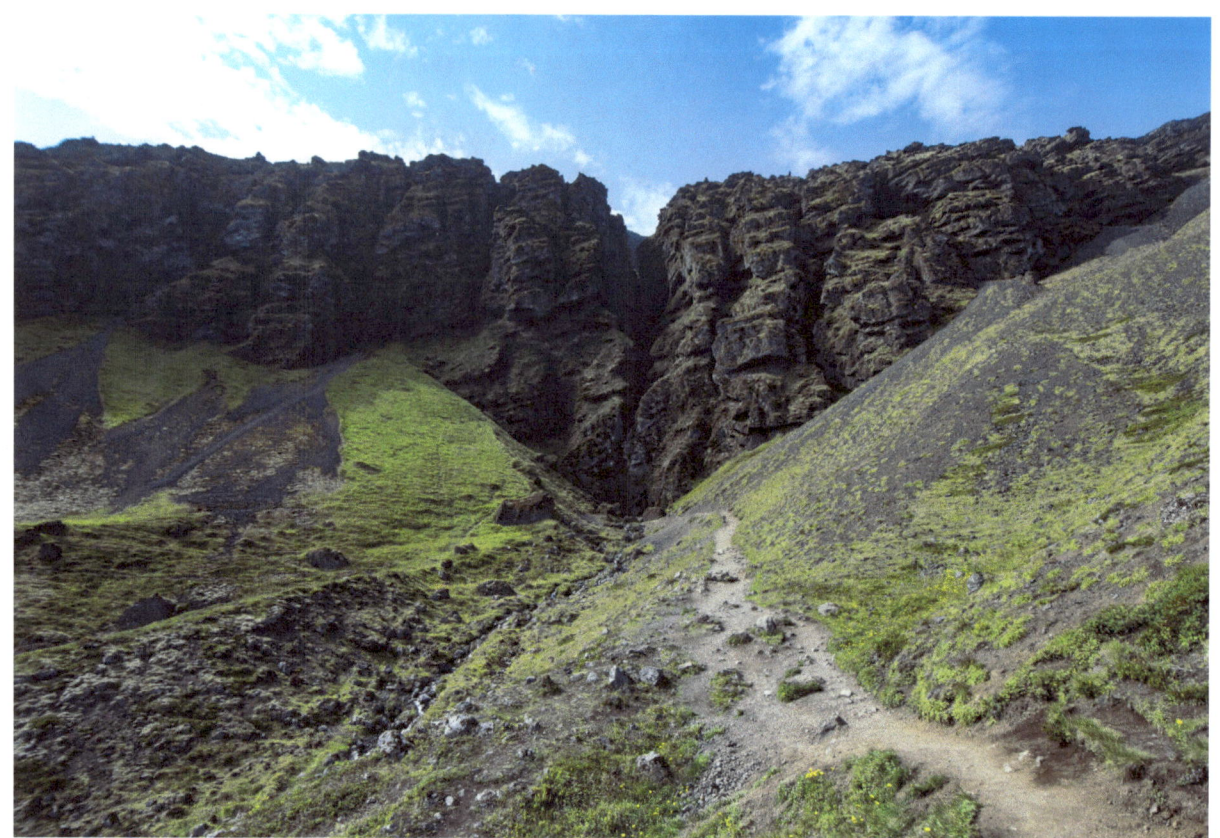

Absolutely Gorgeous Raudfeldsgja Gorge

Thorn In My Stride

There is a thorn in my stride, its keeping me from the best,
this thorn is my pride, I know its a test. I want the underdog to have his day in the sun, and have some fun, but alas, the controlling selfish one ain't no nun. I've found the diva, you know the one who wants her way all the time, does not know any other way, only just the way of her mind. Stealing joy, stealing time, people who enjoy themselves only, ignoring the need, not creating the memories, lonely, These young people that dont know how to share, and care, got off the railroad track, and don't know how to give and live. I am only limited by the boundaries of my mind, and the size of my dreams, but there are joy squashers lying around. I want to check myself, before I wreck myself, knowing the best in me, It's all about love, enjoy the journey, and clearly see, the toughest things are like starring into a glassy lake, all the answers you are looking for are at the bottom, easy as cake, the problem is the pride, the bully, the selfish one, is it you, or is it the reflection in the way, for fun. The person with the greatest need has the least power, the person with the greatest power has the least need. This thorn is persistent.

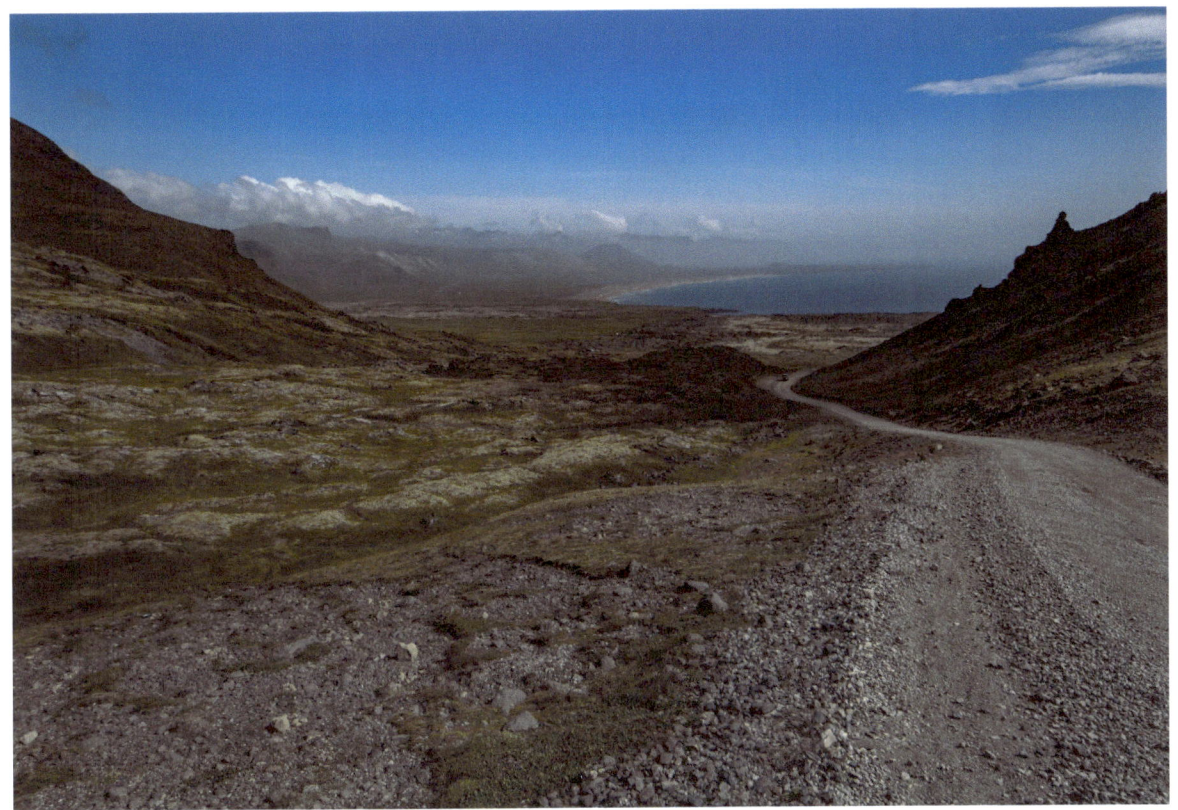

The Only F Road I Drove coming off Snaefellsjokull

Degrees Of The Shuffle

Shades of the shuffle don't want them muffled, the deeper the groove the more the lube dude, sliding fingers over the fret board neck, or on the ivory are the keys oh those tears are crying at how tight the feel, extreme control of the the tactile deal. One slip and you're out of the pocket, maybe next week you're not on the docket, so you know them changes got some pitfalls dangers, are you prepared for the sacrifice, are you prepared for the change of the role of the dice, changing rhythms mesmerizing polyisms, floating and hovering meters, your devilish dance with the groove teeters, seeking the inside yet floating precariously at the outskirts of the outside, conformity without autonomy, compatibility and animinity authenticity groovetastic ability, where else to be then in the groove, no place I'd rather be, but in the midst thought I died when you pop out of this head-trip.

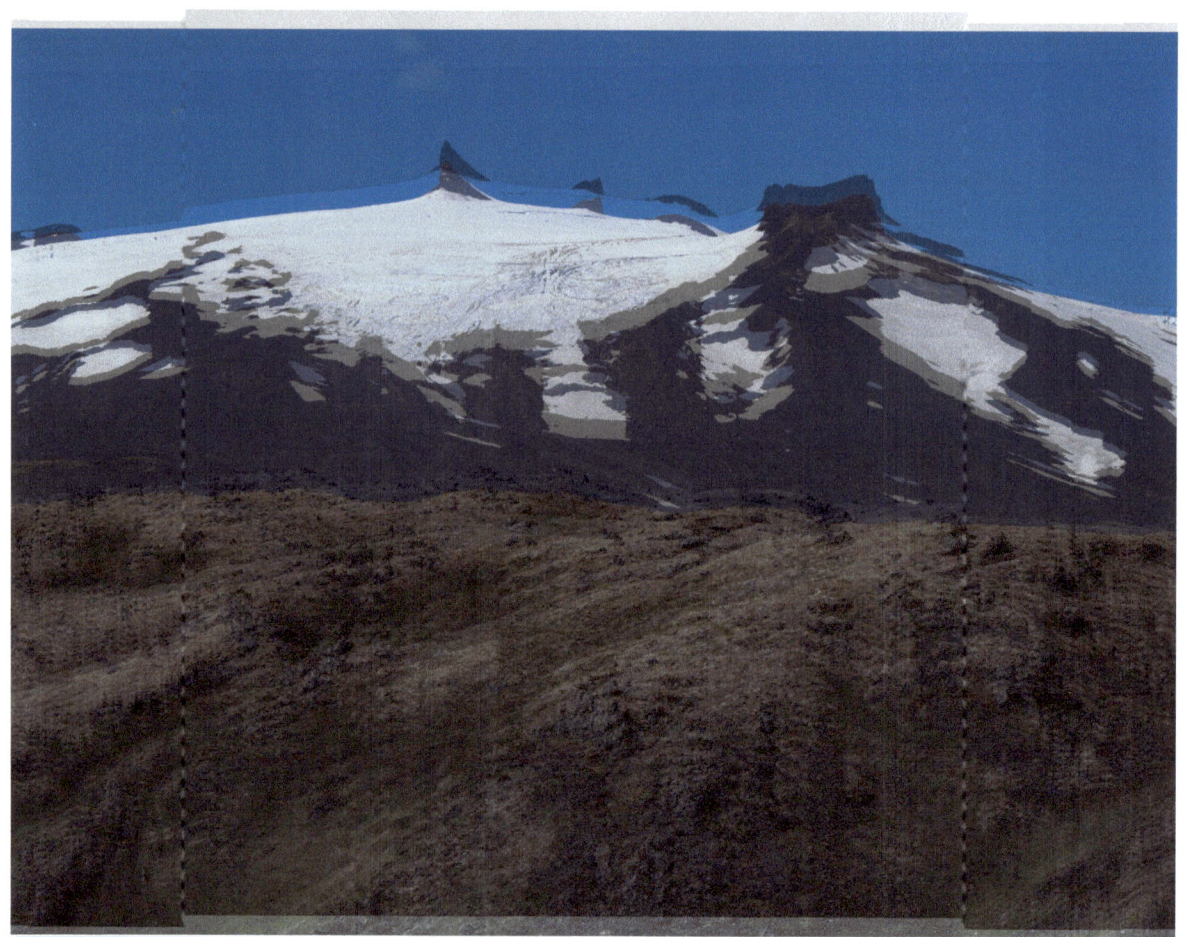

Mount Snaefellsjökull

Unbelievable Love

Sometimes life takes your breath away. You see a sunset, you are surprised by a visit from a loved one, you hear child's laughter, you remember something with fondness. You have to take a deep breath because the feelings that well up in you literally take your breath away. Breathe always, and then there are the moments when you feel like there is not enough air, a job is lost, a diagnosis given, shocking news, when someone so dear is no longer alive. You gasp, you actually have to remind yourself that breathing is not an option, it is necessary. You have to focus and get your grounding and get......some......air. Breathe. At times life may give you whiplash with all of the feelings you experience from one moment to the other. Breathe. Breathing controls our whole bodies, it controls our functions, we need it to survive.

My experience is that this part of our created-ness is also a function that God uses as a way to pace us. Breathe. Breathe, just breathe. Come and rest at my feet and be, just as Chaos calls, but all you really need is to take it in fill your lungs, the peace of God that overcomes, just breathe. So let your weary spirit rest, lay down what's good and find what's best, just breathe. Taste that food, climb that mountain, run that marathon, make that art! Sing, dance, create!! Spread your exuberance! Let your enthusiasm fill us with delight and inspiration! Love, no matter what.

I've got the sun shining down on me with an angel in my heart, that keeps me and uplifts the soul of my heart. A heart is full of love, waves hits our feet as you dance, and pay it forward, do an act of kindness, don't listen to the belittling one, care for the poor, feed the hungry, give water to the thirsty, clothe the sick, visit the prisoner, love thy neighbor as myself, love God with all my heart soul and strength, that every very human is equally loved by our Maker. No earthly power can ever take away or change the hope I have in my Savior.

I will not die an unlived life. I will not live in fear of falling or catching fire. I choose to inhabit my days, to allow my living to open me, to make me less afraid, more accessible, to loosen my heart, until it becomes a wing, a torch, a promise. I choose to risk my significance; to live so that which, came to me as seed goes to the next as blossom and that which came to me as blossom, goes on as fruit.

I took a beautiful journey to the country of Iceland in the summer of 2019, and want to share the story of this journey. Prior to traveling, I had lots of rescheduling problems with Icelandair due to Boeing 737 max problems, but thankfully Expedia was able to solve them for me. I was ultimately further delayed into Boston by summer rains, and missed the flight to Reyjavik by minutes. I had a day to spend in Boston, and I made the most of it. I saw a local artist escape from a straight jacket upside-down, and took the public rails to the museum of art. I also saw the old north church and spent some time in the marketplaces and local culture. Boston really is old America.

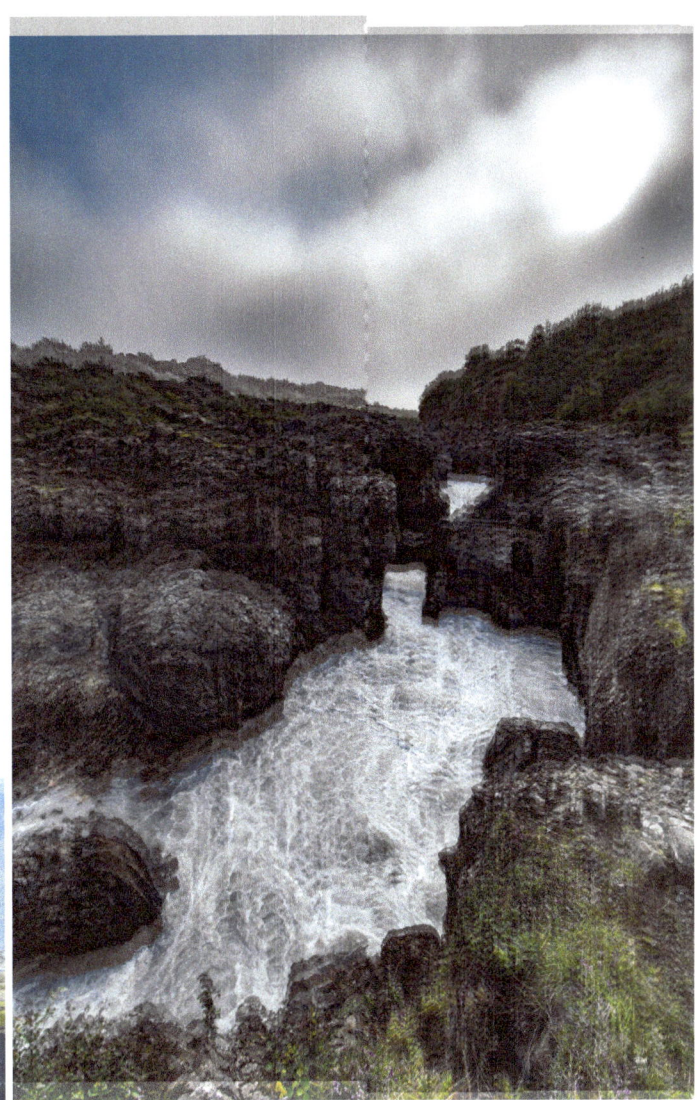

Hraunfoss Falls

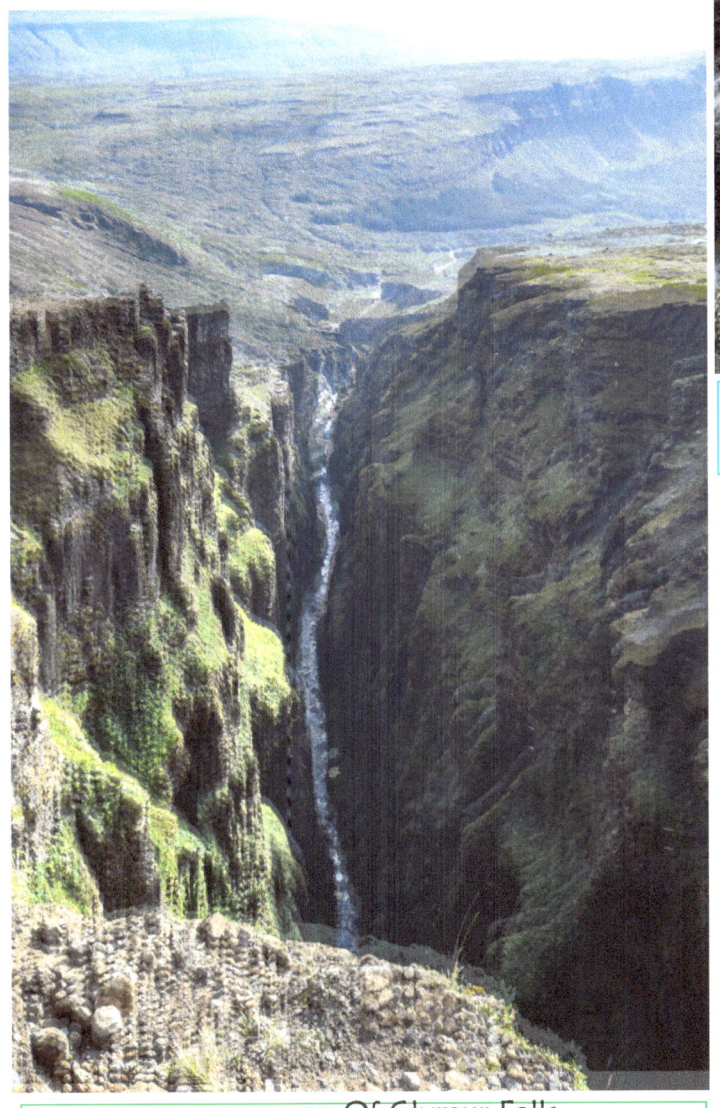

The Canyon Of Glymur Falls

On the 767—200 airplane I was served by these these really huge Icelandic stewardressess, and thankfully the airline gave me a whole row of seats to myself. I arrived at this small airport and ate a hearty, and ultimately deathly English breakfast, before finding ACE rental car for a Skoda Octavia car. I had lost a day so I scrambled over to Gullfoss, Haifoss and Seljalandsfoss for some time with the peace of the waterfalls. I believe the gas prices to be somewhere around $6.5 U.S. dollars a gallon, but of course prices are in Krona dollars, and liters in Iceland.

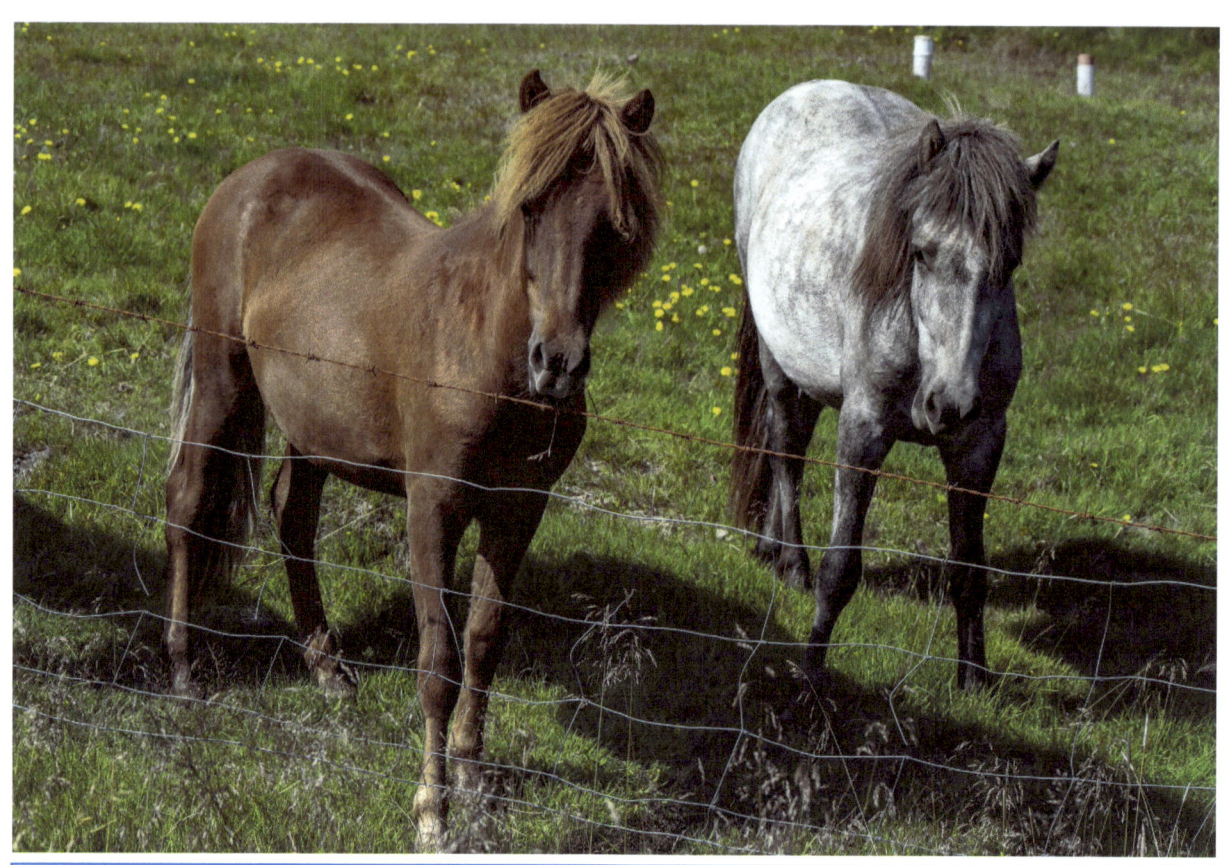

Beautiful Icelandic Horses

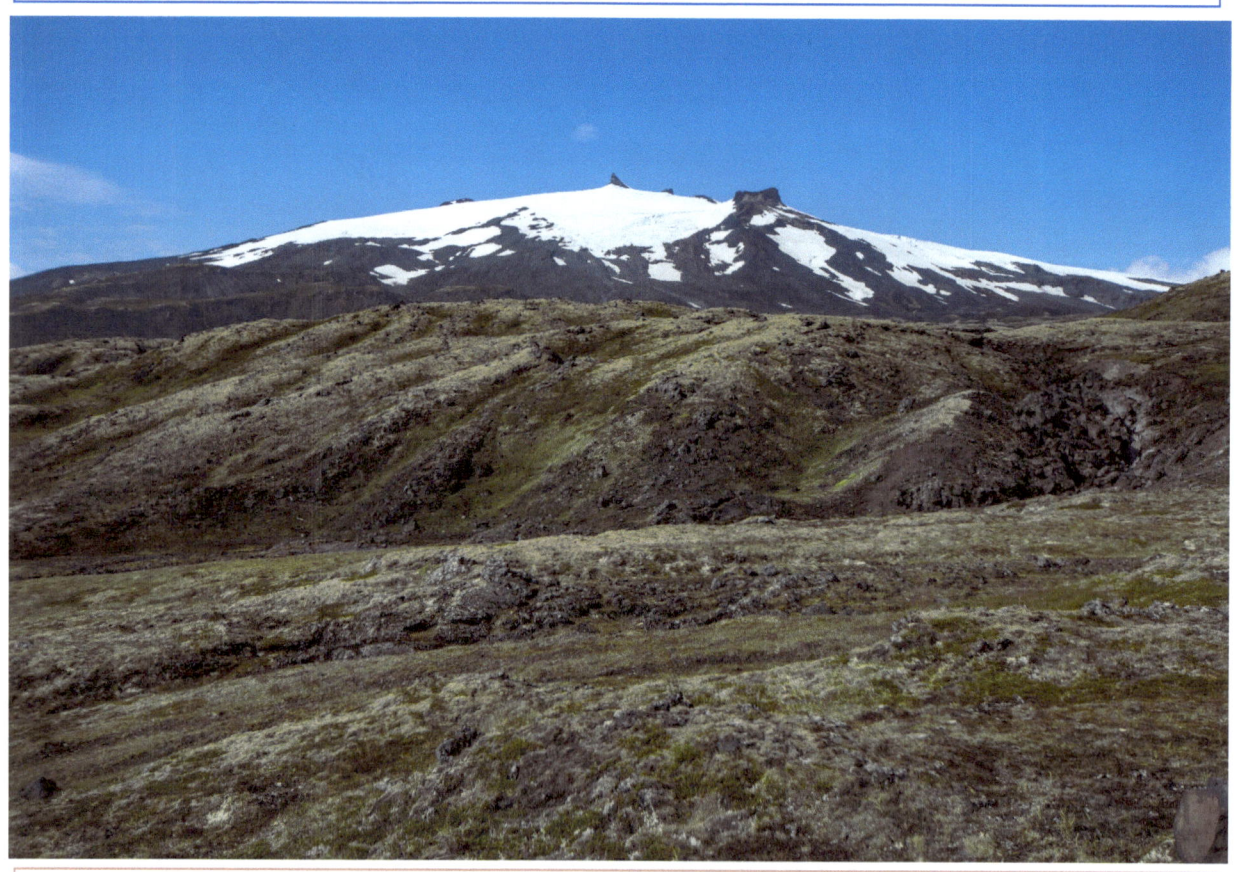

Mount Snaefellsjokull

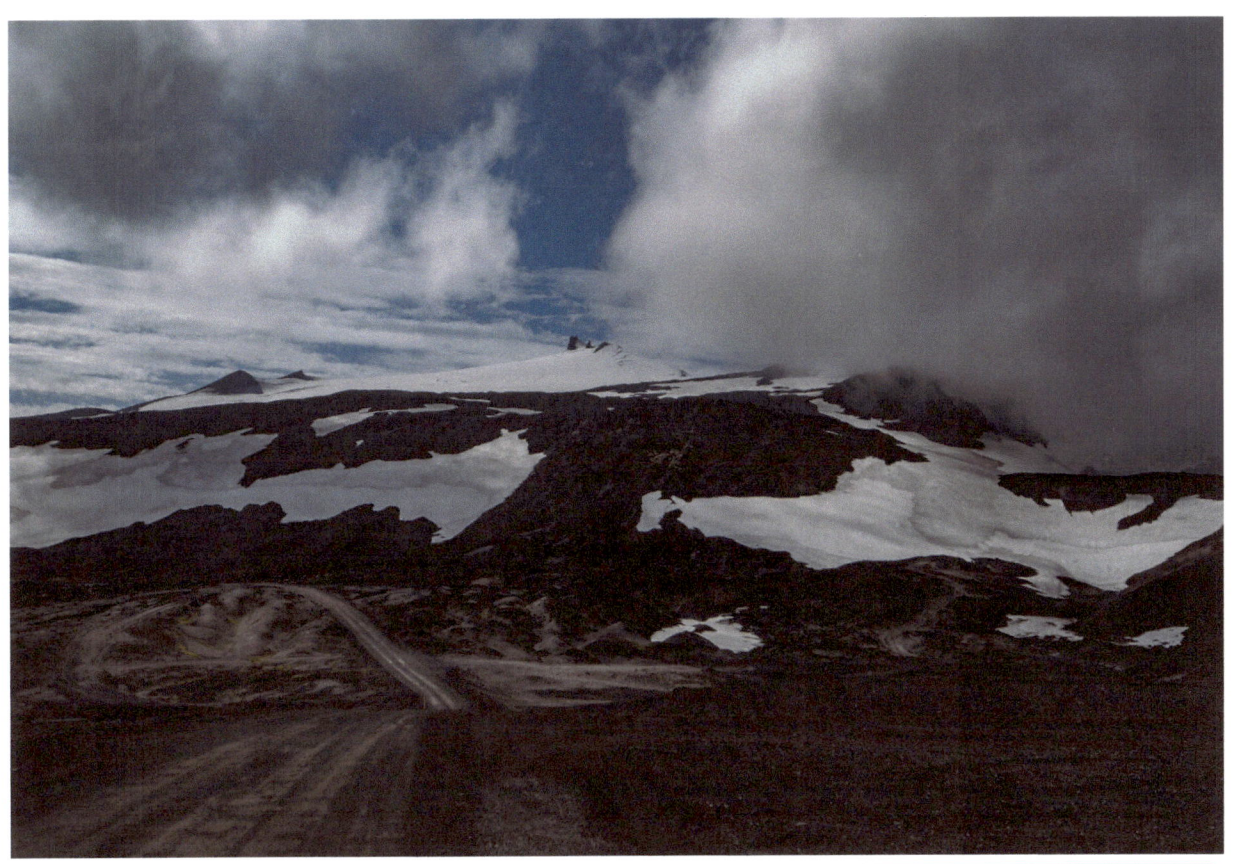
Mount Snaefellsjokull

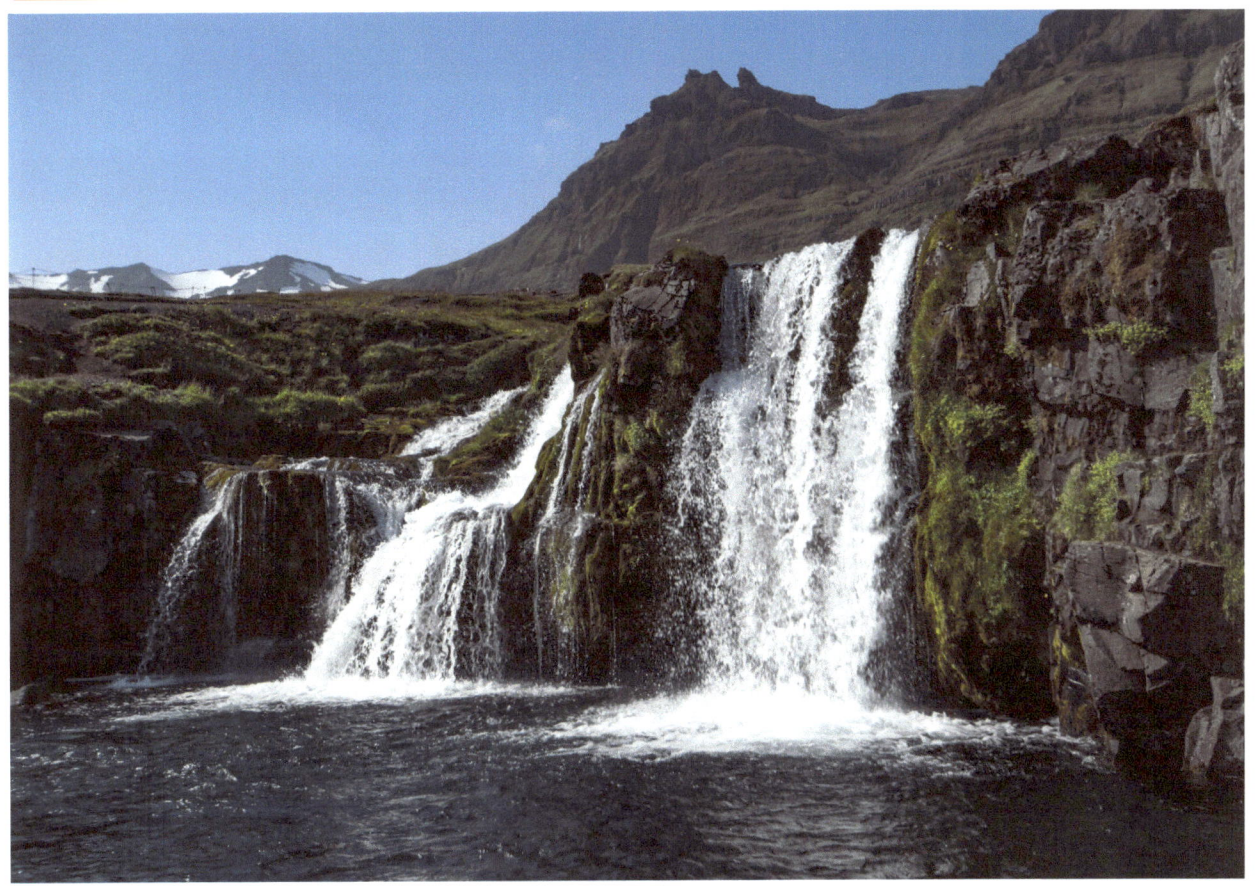
Dynjandi Falls

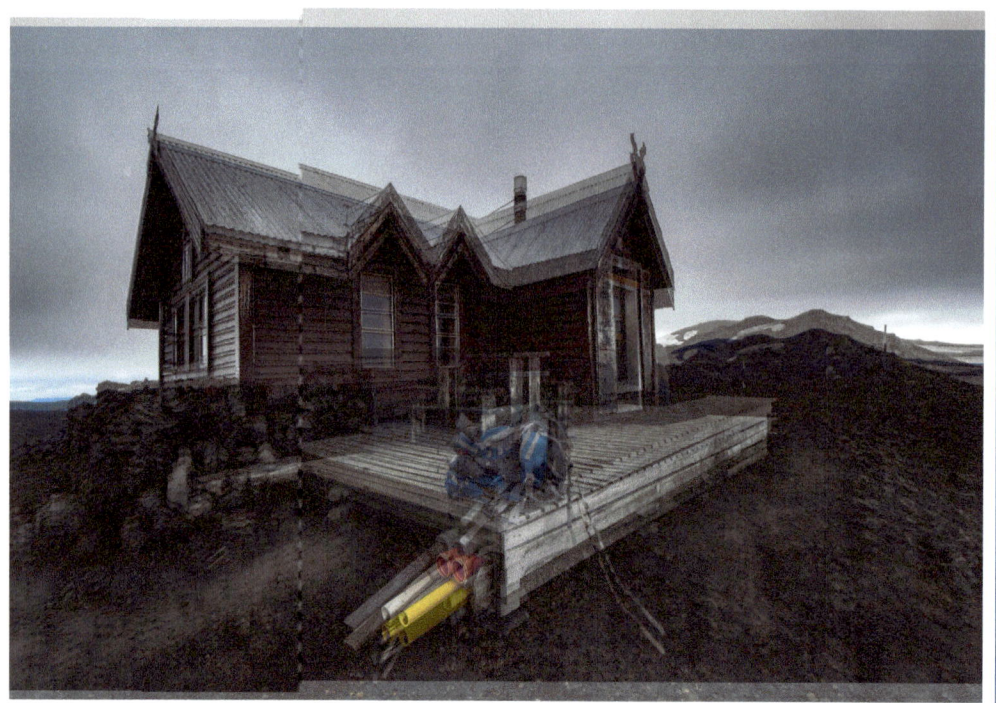

Mountain Hut at Fimmvorduhals

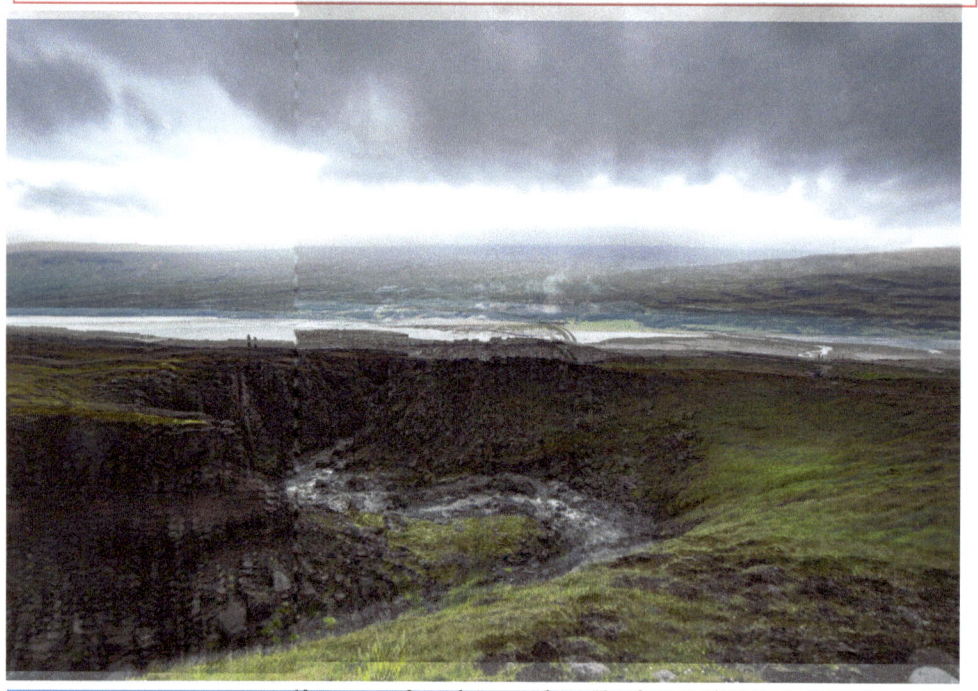

Kirkjufoss Falls overlooking the Egilsstadir Region

I ate some wheat because I thought I bought some granola, but could not read the labeling, suffered some problems and recovered. I found the road to Gullfoss ok, but traveling to Haifoss was really tough on a gravel road. I had been warned about windshield damage and car body damages from sharp volcanic rock, and had a $3500 deposit. I found an unbelievable amount of tourists at Seljalandfoss, and parked at the nearby Gljufrabui by mid-afternoon. I really enjoyed this beautiful walk behind the falls. I settled into Snostra Hostel for the evening and made some vegetables and salmon for supper and found the hostel very empty and quiet.

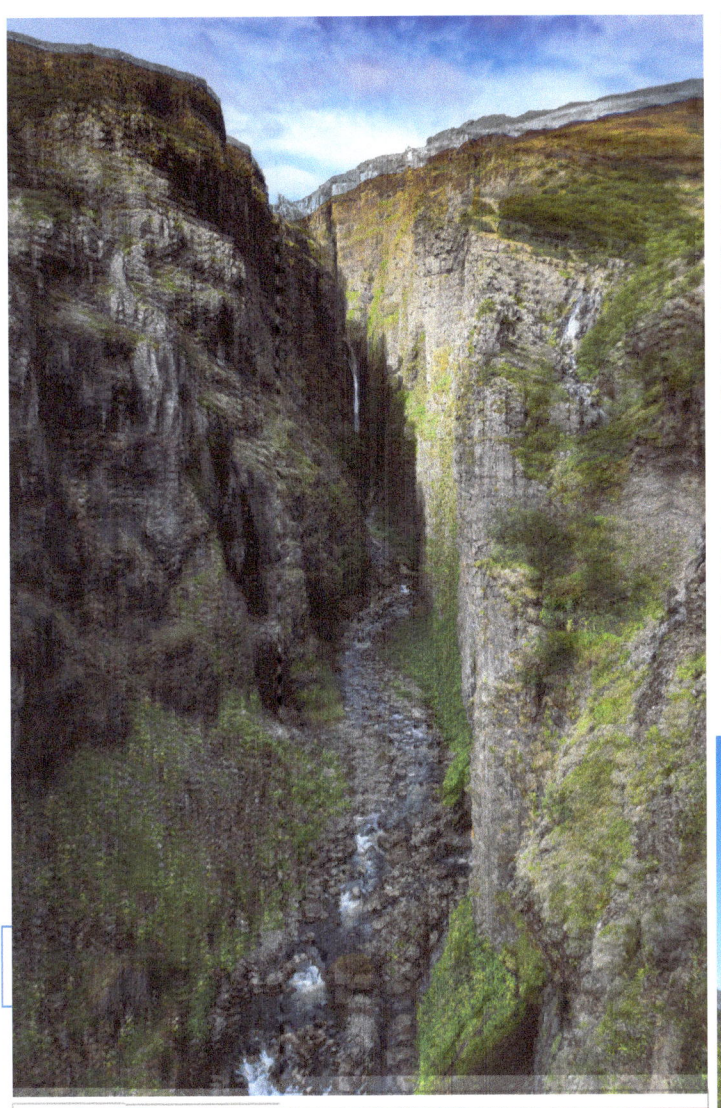

Glymur Falls

My late/delayed arrival means my 2 day backpack was next on the agenda, and I traveled to Skogar to go up 3500 feet to a backcountry hut at Fimmvorduhals hut. This was quite simply a gorgeous hike, one of my top and most amazing journeys ever, and on melting glaciers. Up at the hut, I played what the people called Chinese poker with some Americans from Georgia and also some Spaniards. The warden was a grumpy old man with his lover, and the hut was really old, but warm and well ventilated even with 16 people, and window open overnight. The fog rolled in during the evening hours before bed, and whenever the sun set. I dozed off and I wondered whether I'd ever get out of there. It was a tiring hike up to the top for me at that time, and kind of reminded me of the Cascades.

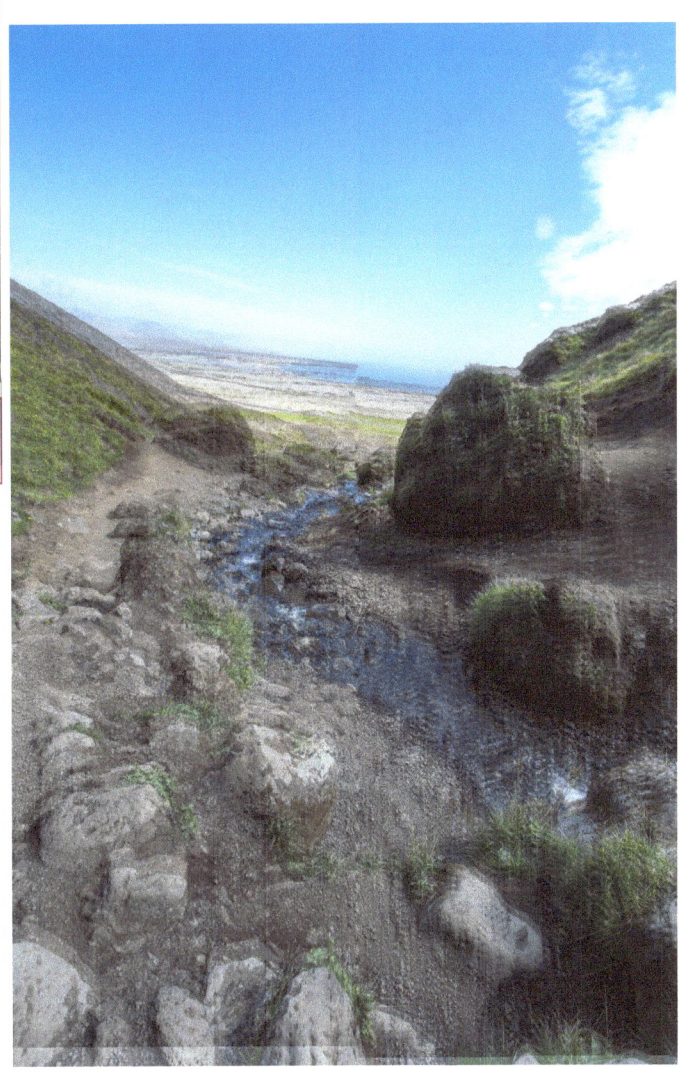

Raudfeldsgja Gorge

The sun goes down to the horizon at 6 pm and sits there until around 11pm where it sets and then get up at 3:30 am so it was kind of hard to sleep without some sheets blocking the light. I accidentally left my fleece jacket and waterbottle at the smaller falls overnight and camp back in the morning for them. Thankfully they drive on right side, Ok the correct side of road, and roads in general were excellent here. I found most people speak English, and the hosts at hostel, were Polish, with some French and German also. My late arrival meant I had to abandon plans for Blahnukur and Landmannalaugar, but I can go back and do a longer backpack one day.

I hiked down and out and had a transitional day from Fimmvorduhals to Skogar over to Hofn for a hostel by 9pm. I found the parking lot extremely full with tourists buses when I came out I stopped at several places. This short hike to Fjadrargljufur canyon was absolutely beautiful. I also stopped in the National Park of Vatnajokull and found a bunch of information for next visit about ice caves and snowmobile tours. There seem to be a number of trails and jump off points going to features in the park, but it was raining and not great visibility so I took a short hike to Svartifoss falls in the fog and drizzle and headed to Diamond Beach.

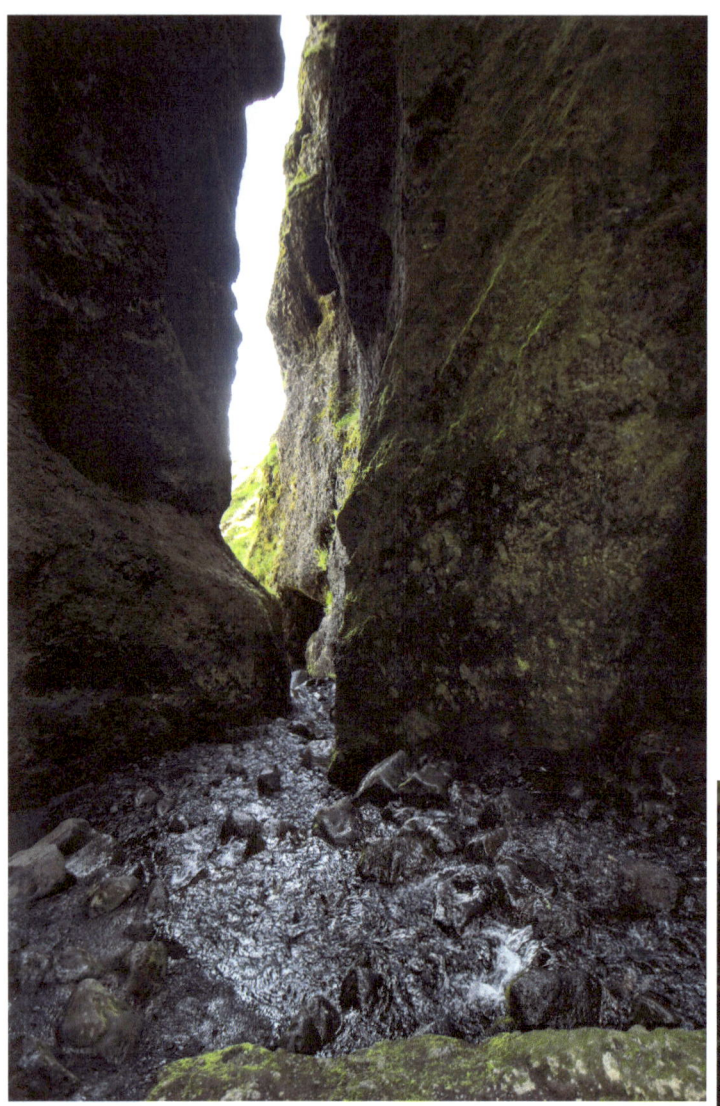

Raudfeldsgja Gorge

I felt truly horrible in the morning with a beast of a cold from some European traveler that I have never experienced. It took a good 6 days to rid of this beast of the an illness. I was encouraged by this beautiful exquisite hike. Trails were a mix of anchored snow posts and open sections crossing snowy glaciers. There were some rocky sections and well maintained dirt trails, and simply absolutely amazing scenery. I had some freeze dried meals from Mountain House of chicken fiesta and Italian style pepper steark, and made on glacial waters. Although not a home cooked meal, they really hit the spot. I got up fairly early and climb down to continue my counter-clockwise Iceland assault.

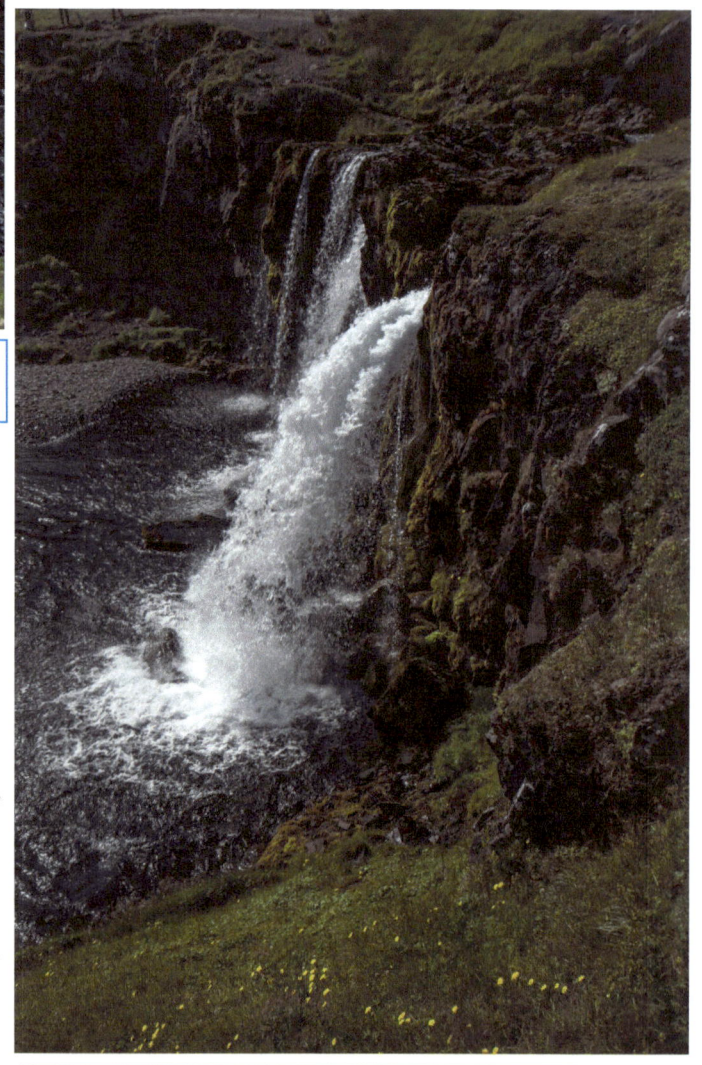

Kirkjufellsfoss Falls

I drove east and found the history of a woman who collected rocks named Petra in a town near Stodvarfjordu. I paid for the museum which her family runs now that she has passed and some of the most beautiful and colorful rocks I have ever seen were on display.

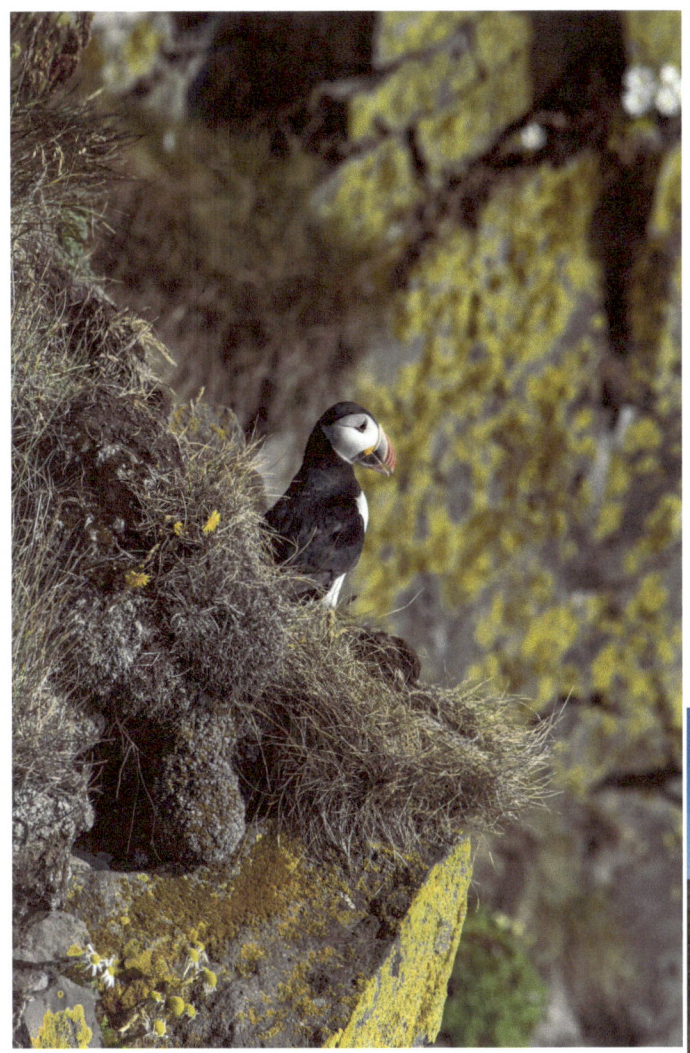

Puffins in Latrabjarg

At Diamond Beack, I visited three sides of the river, but really only got out of the car for short visits. It was very cold at 35 F and raining. This area is where the Glacier melts and drains out with car sized icebergs floating down the river and landing on the shores. The weather was deteriorating in the shadow of the glacier and visibility was poor. I somehow found my was to Hofn hostel with minutes to spare by 9pm for the night. The staff was waiting and closed the office soon after that. I made some dinner of fresh vegetables and salmon from a grocery store obtained earlier in the day.

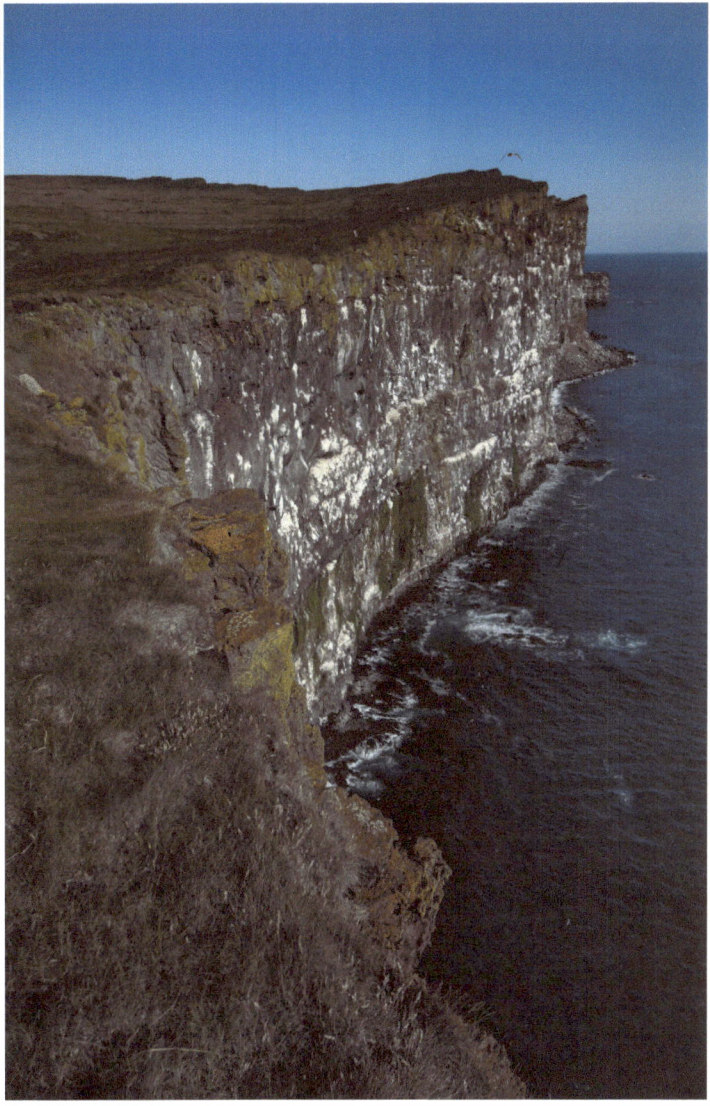

Latrabjarg Cliffs

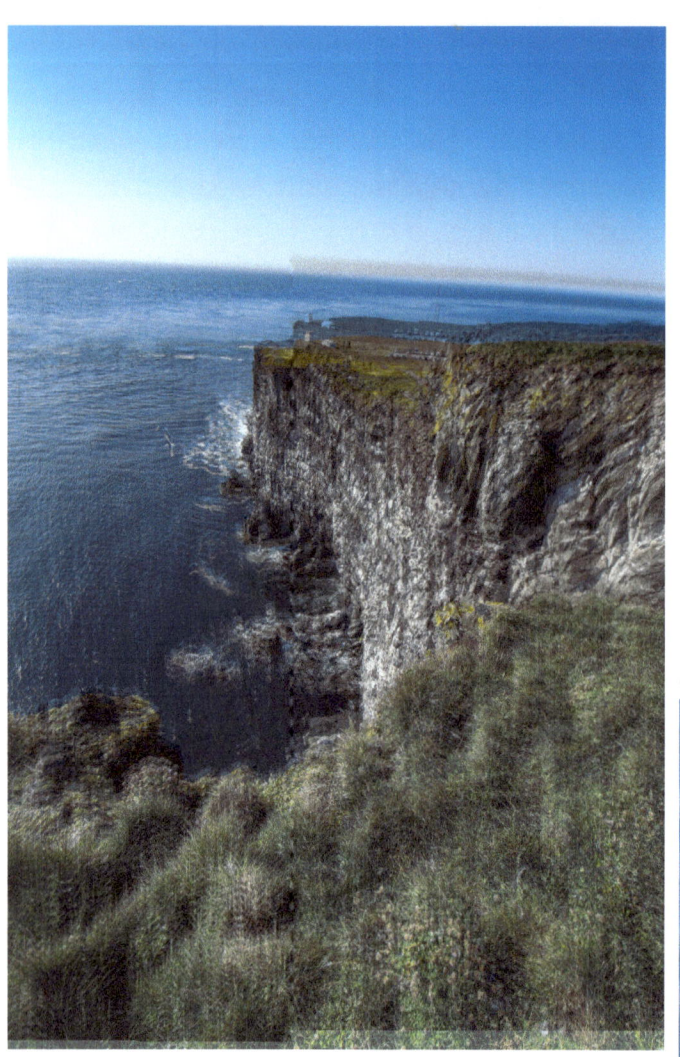

I could not find a lot of information about this area prior to visit so had a helpful host recommended Asbrygi Canyon, which I had also read about. This was a fun day travelling from Egilsstadir to the Hild hostel. With weather in the 80's and beautiful sunny day, it was a beautiful hike in and up to and along the rim of Asbrygi canyon. I travelled to the North Sea and also saw a waterfall into the ocean. The expansive views of plains and hills heading up to the north sea were extremely impressive, and completely vacant of any civilization.

Latrabjarg Cliffs

The traveling from Hofn to Egilsstadir was the most difficult of the entire journey with dirt gravel roads, and almost zero viability in the fog. This road was seriously tough and one of the most difficult of any road I have ever driven, and right up there with driving mountain highways in white-out conditions in the hills of West Virginia. It was not cold just really sticky humid, but not at all like Ohio. It had some moments of clearing at a beautiful falls called Kirkjufoss, and also on a local pass at Fardagafoss and Gufufoss. I settled in and rested early at a families home called Mjoanes with Elsa and Maggie. I talked with the owners and played a little with a beautiful pure bred Icelandic sheep puppy dog with a huge coat.

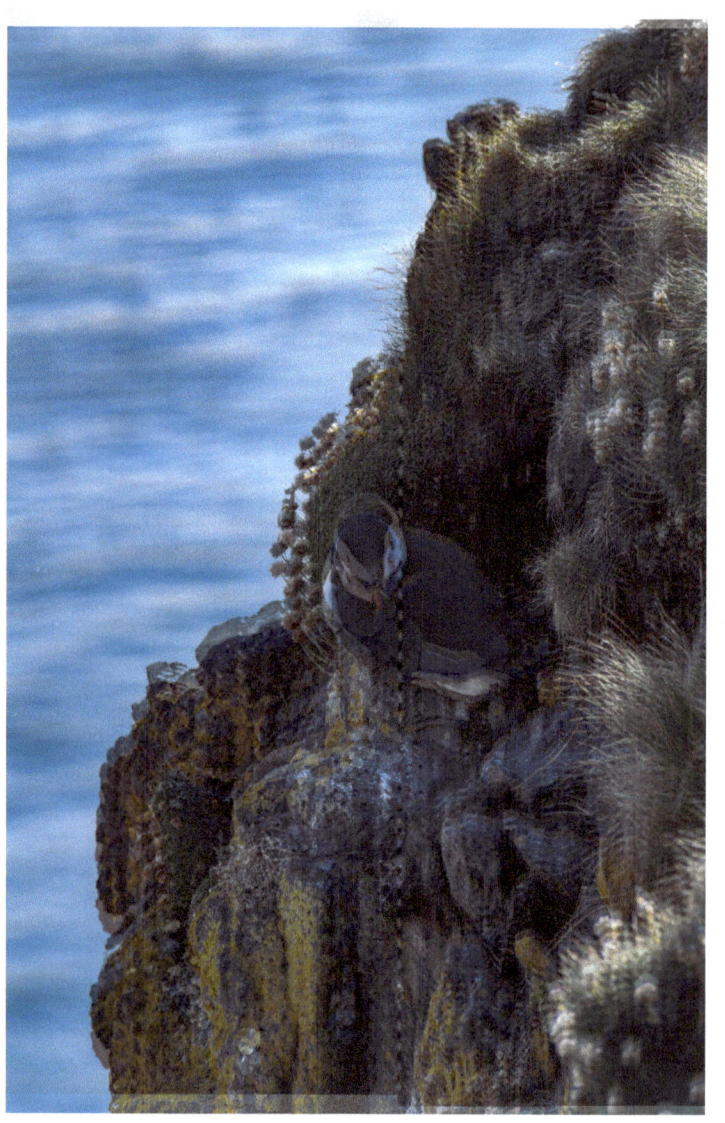

Puffins in Latrabjarg

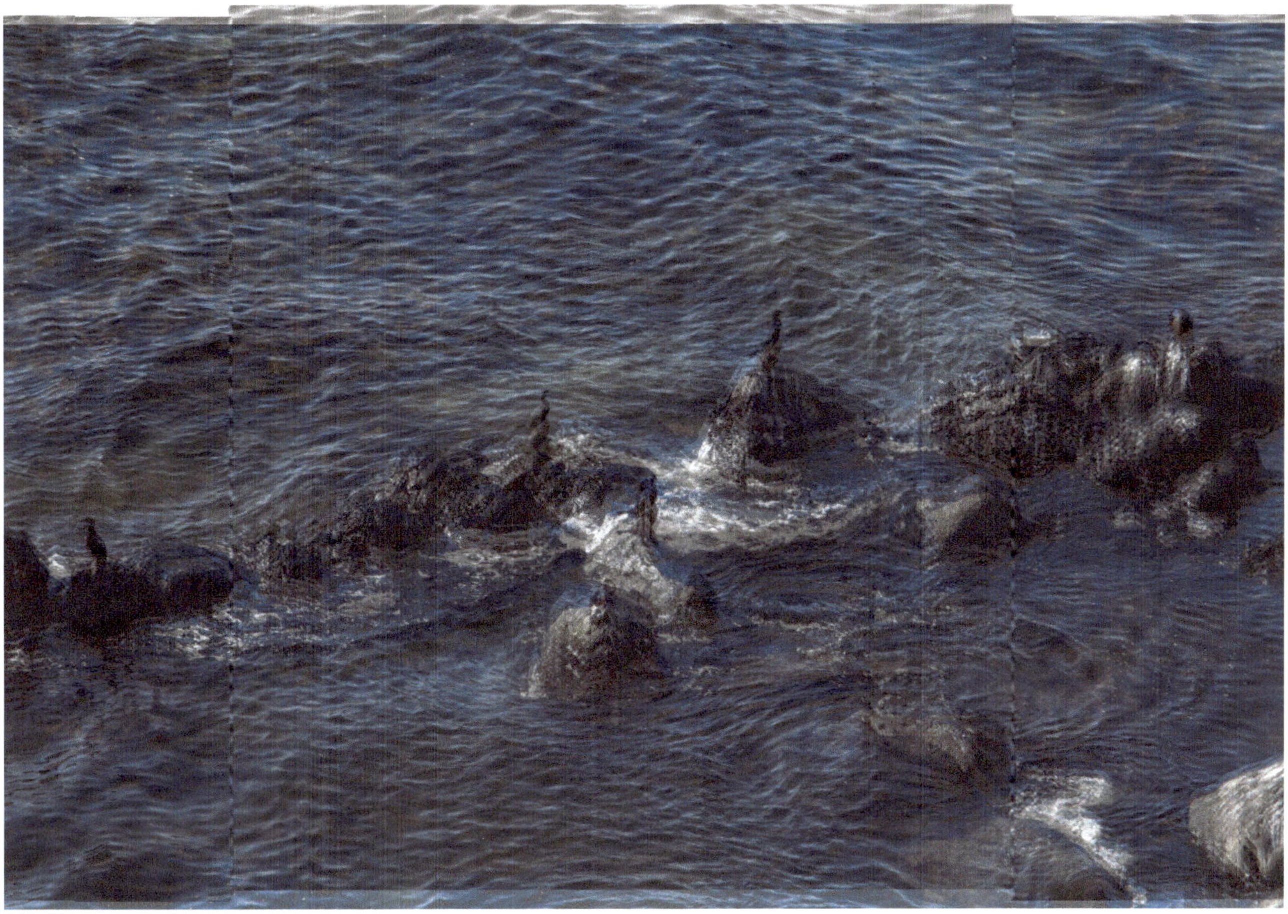

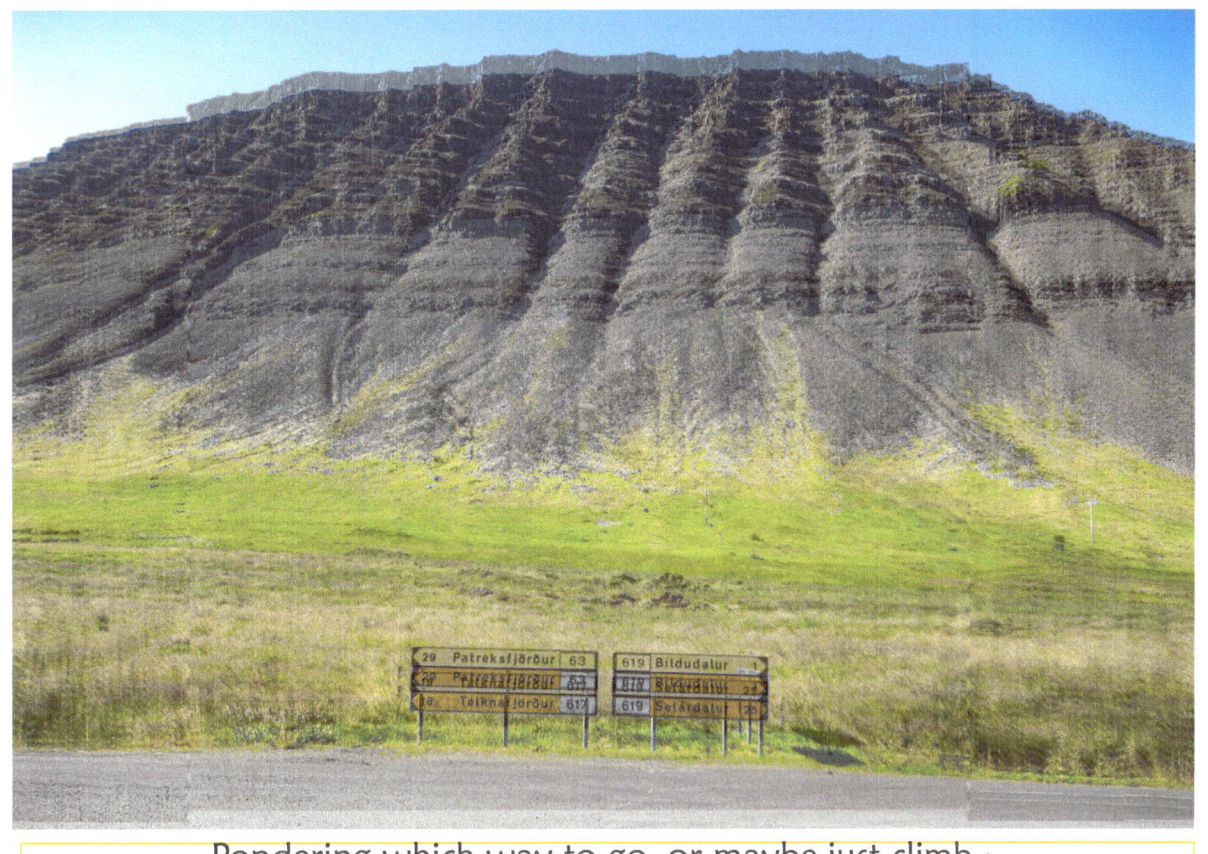

Cliffs to the North Sea off Latrabjarg

Pondering which way to go; or maybe just climb it

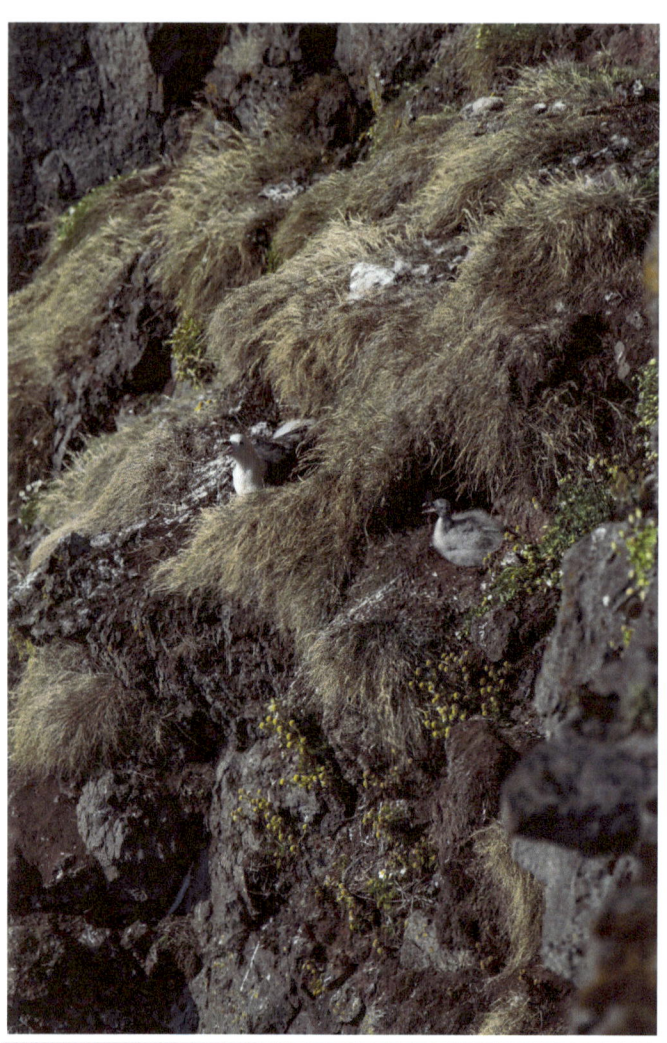

Birds on cliffs of Latrabjarg

Feeling tired I spent the day in Akureki Iceland town center with a bad cold, maybe even flu. So I rested up the enjoyed the culture and found a wool sweater extremely well made and probably should have purchased it. I visited the church with trapestries, stained glass, the contemporary art museum, and gift shops. The art museum was displaying natural painting similar to Portland Oregon artists, and also Banff art museum as well as Europeans influences. I also marveled at an outdoor botanical gardens established in 1909, and how it even exists in this seemingly inhospitable terrain. I never did see a forest in this country and I believe they used all the wood because most homes were made of concrete.

At the Sellfoss and Detifoss there was an insane amount of water going over the falls. There was also an extremely hot thermal area called Namafjall Hverir right off the road. It was full of sulfur smell and difficult to breath if you were caught in the midst of the vapor. This area has a lot of cracked earth lava formations, and natural caves, and I really should go back for some of them. It reminded me of craters of the moon in Wyoming. I cooked some chicken thighs and vegetables in a busy Hostel at Hild.

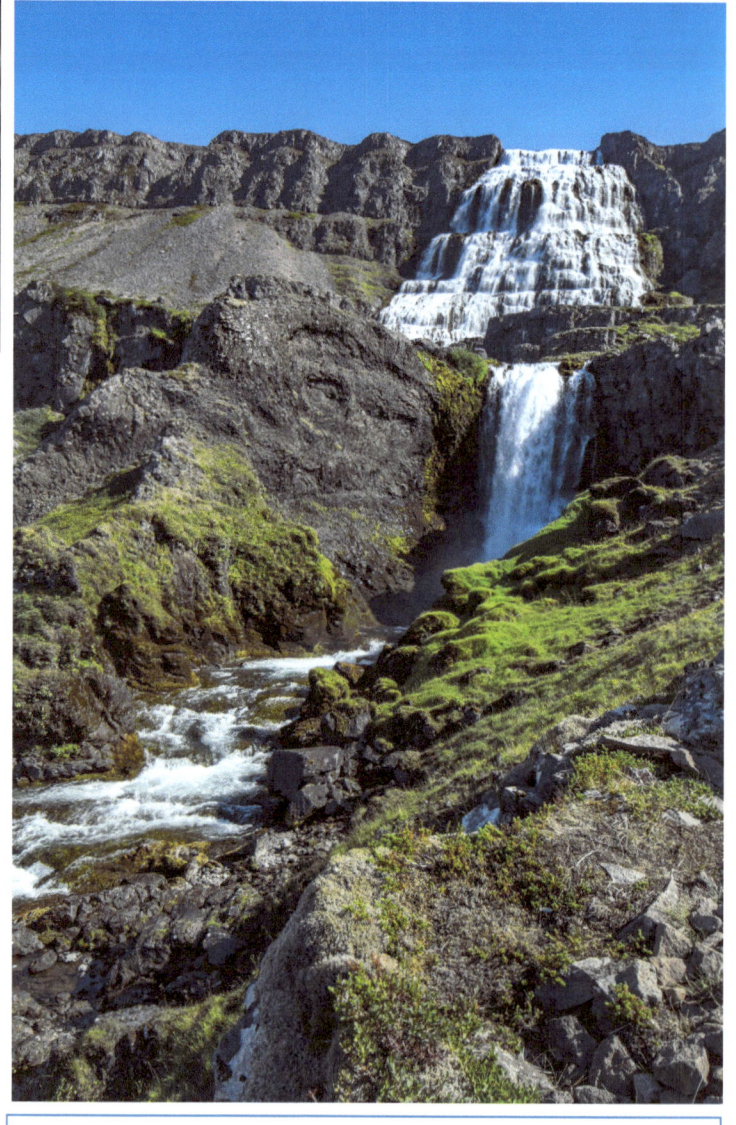

Dynjandi Falls

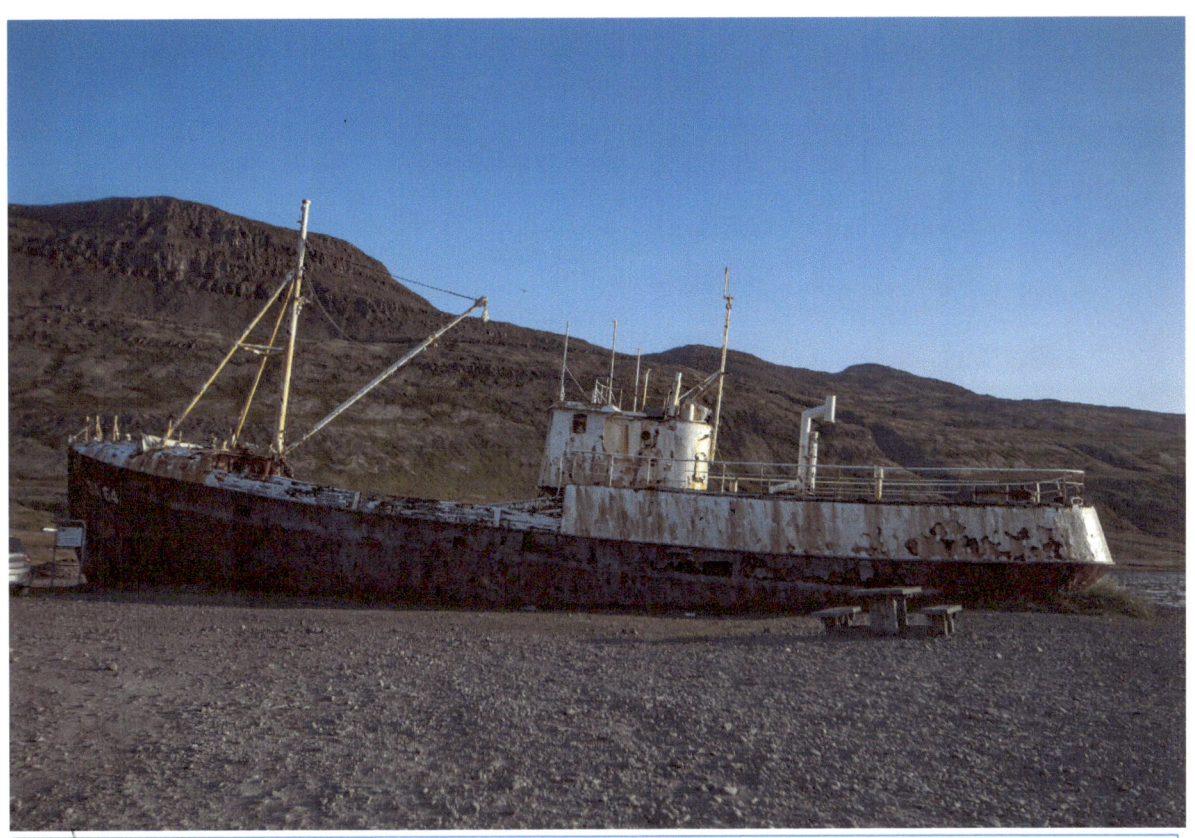

Seriously Grounded Ship in the West Fjords

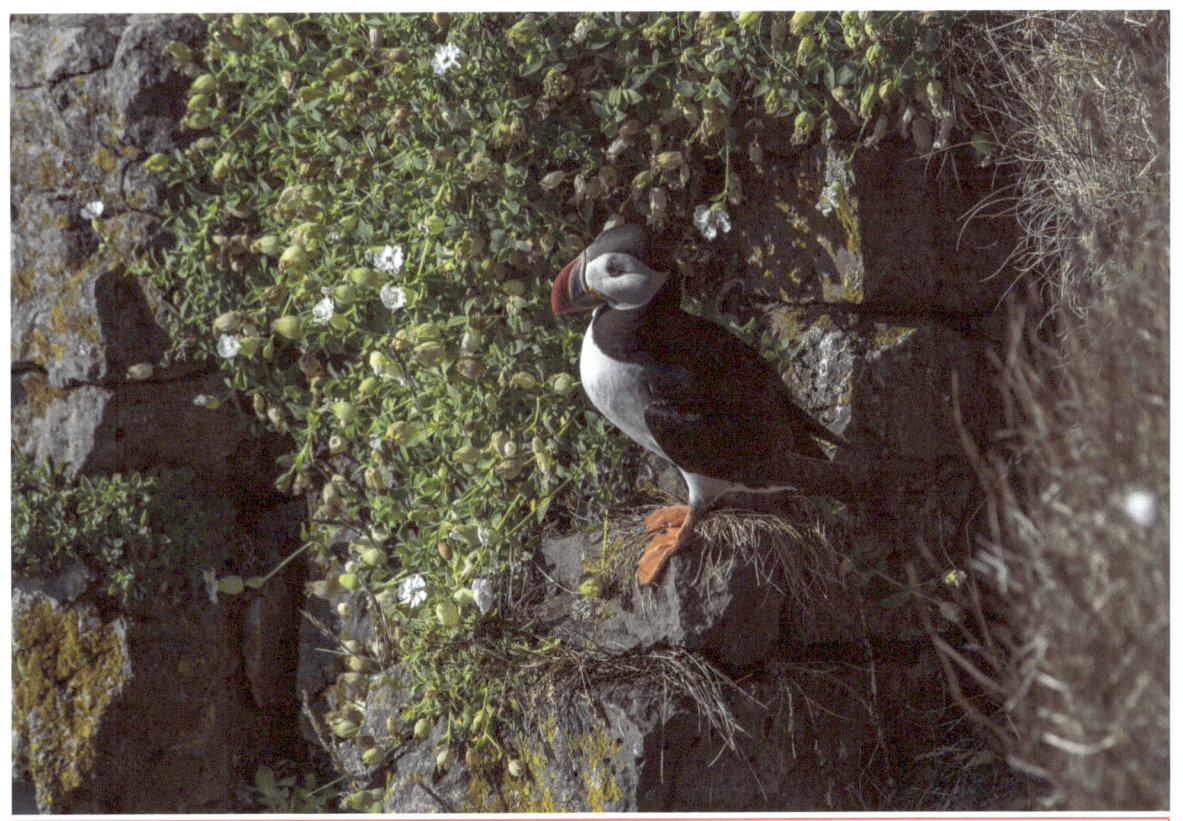

Puffins in Latrabjarg

I took very long travel day tomorrow from Akureyki to Reyholar hostel and then kept going to Dynjandi waterfall and Latrabjarg Puffin cliffs and also Raudissandur beach. Dynjandi waterfall was probably the best in all of Iceland for its sheer size and beauty. I had a 200 zoom lens on my Nikon camera with me so taking pictures of Puffins was joyful, but also a challenge. Small little birds who fly but mostly glide. Latrabjarg cliff were similar in size to the white cliffs of Dover in size, but very much different rock. This was the farthest north I have ever been at the 65th parallel. The expansive beach of Raudissandur is like the Michigan upper peninsula. I saw a lot of campers down at the beach, but I simply did not have enough time at this beach. The white sand beach lured me to stay but I needed to press on at nearly 9pm before arriving back at the Hostel at nearly 1130 pm. There was no one available to check in, but I note had been left for me with instructions.

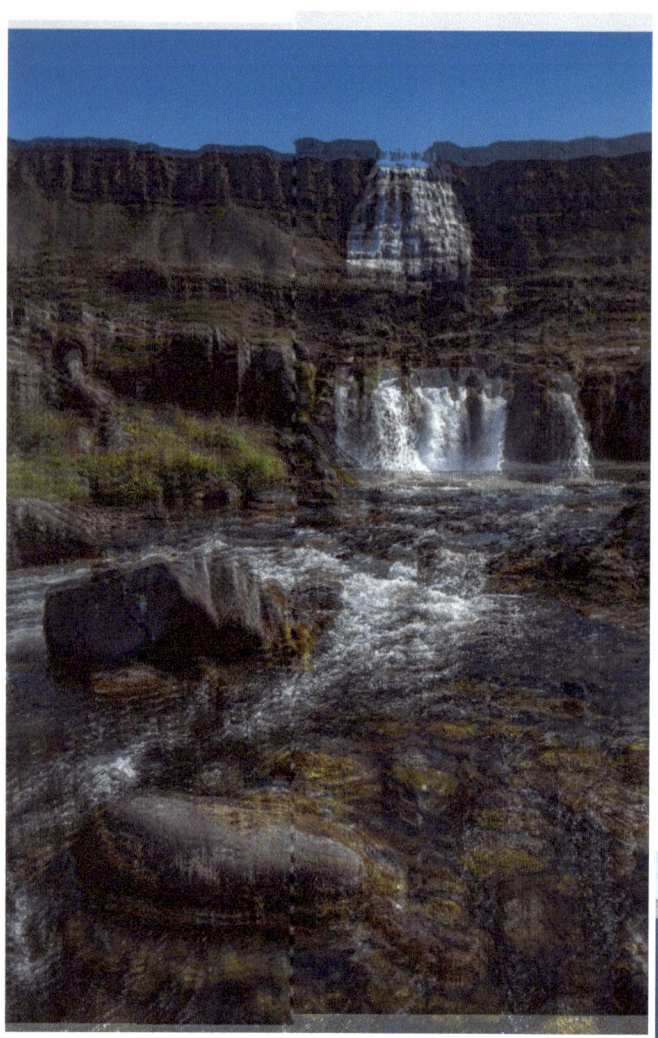

Dynjandi Falls

A morning visit to a waterfall of Godafoss was fun, and with the area near it having cracked earth from recent lava. I also took a loop drive north of Akureki through hillsides and long carved car tunnels, and huge expansive valleys and hillsides. I found an abandoned cottage in a valley all made of stone. It had all the windows broken, and roof collapsing which was fascinating. I walked inside and found a 3 inch door of wood from an old time in history. Someone lives here years ago and maybe the house could be salvagabled, but it would take a lot of work. On this loop drive I stopped at a pullout and scrambled down to the streambed for a break. I did not seek this but encountered a sheep with horns who stood his ground and protected his family, and I had to scramble off trail a little to avoid being charged at.

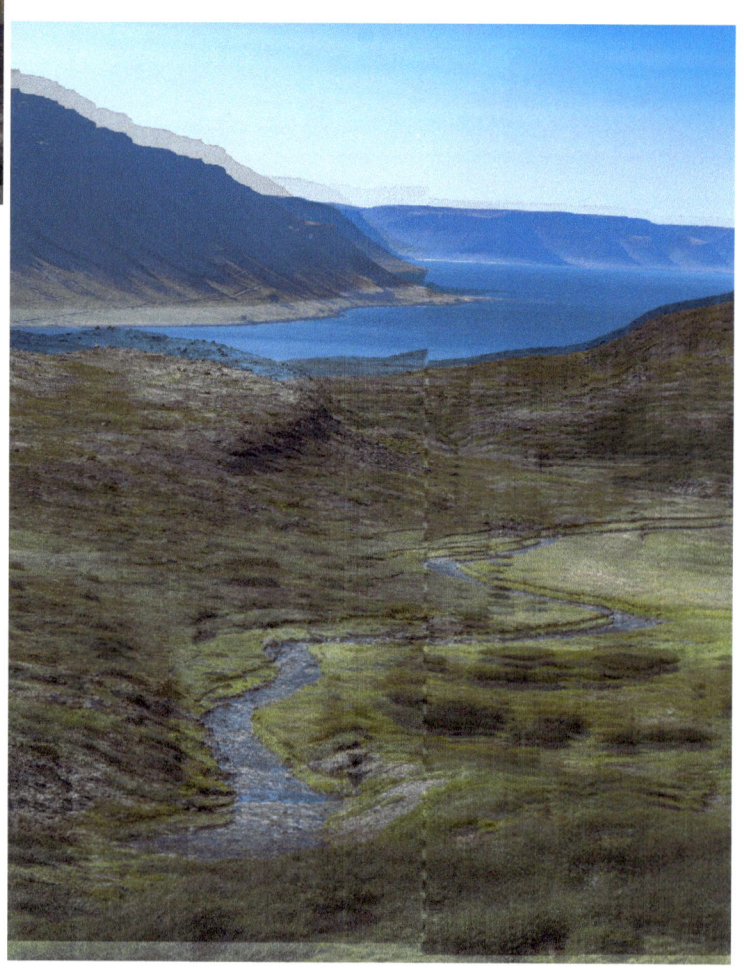

The Endless West Fjords

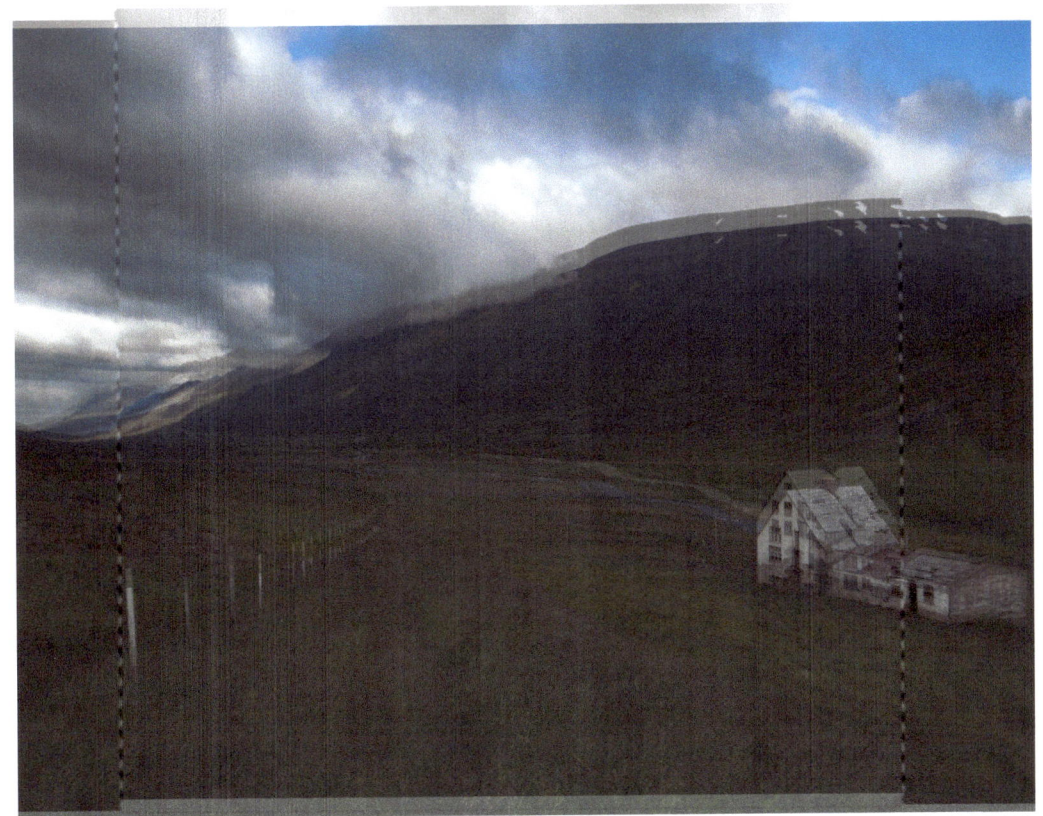

Abandoned Farmhouse Outside of Akureyri

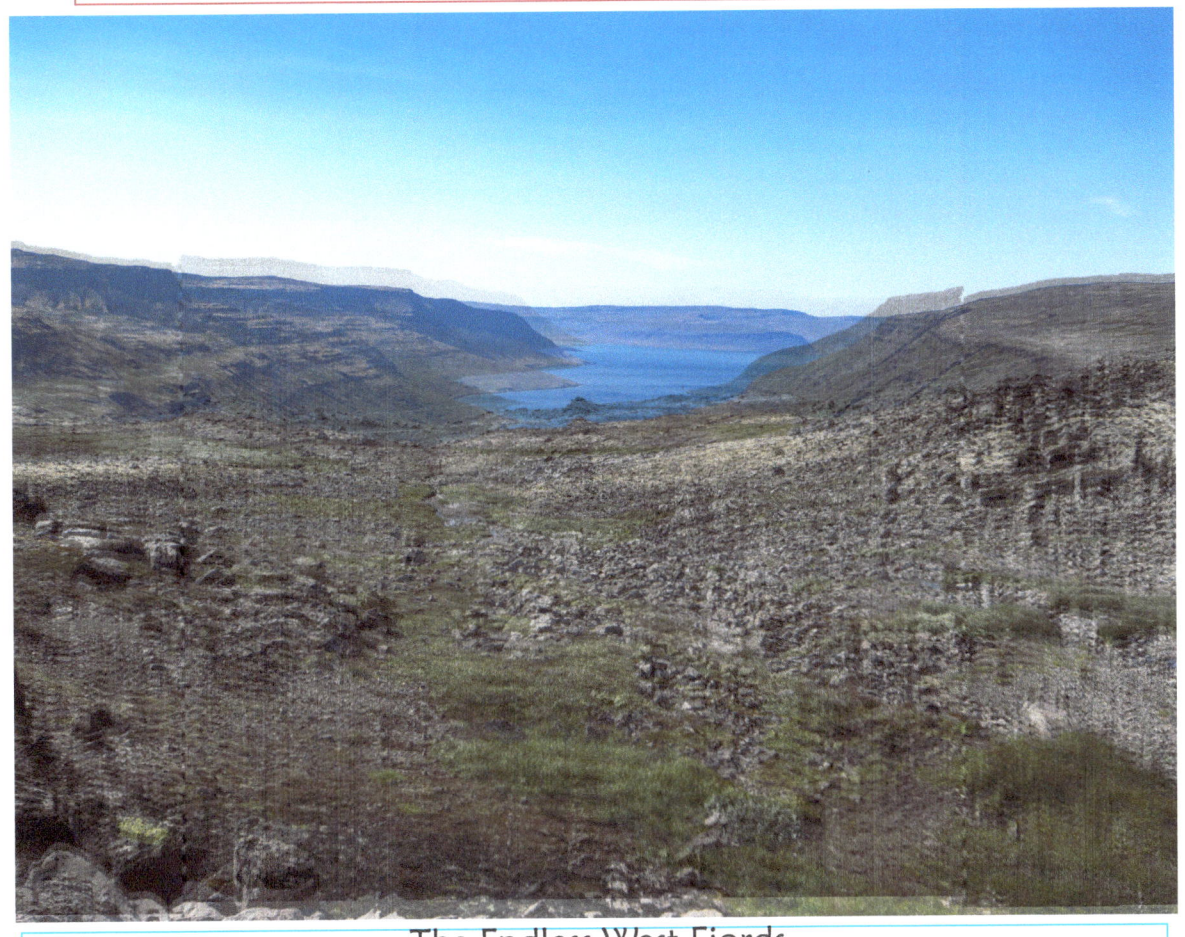

The Endless West Fjords

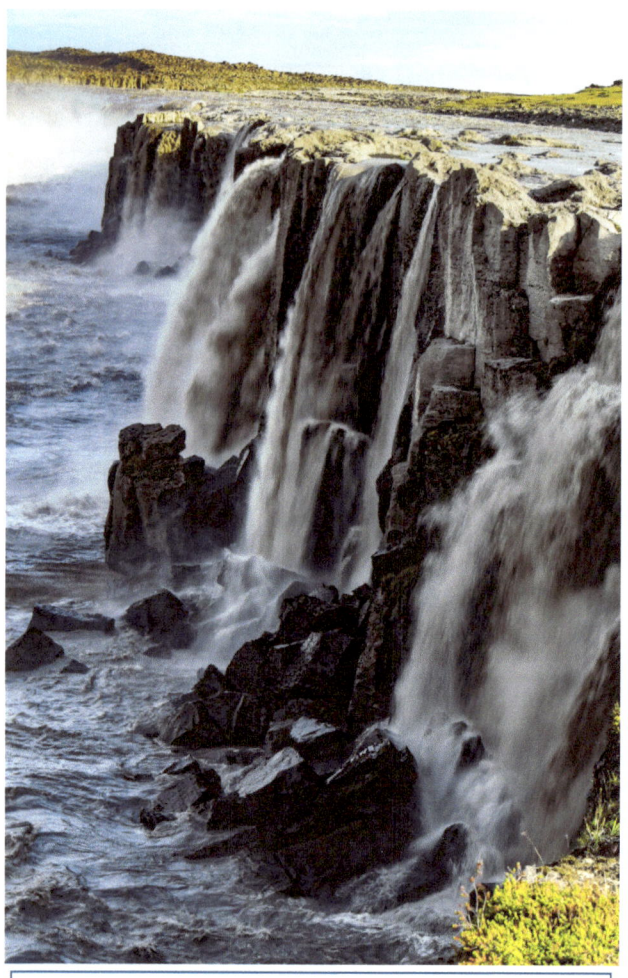

Side Falls of Godafoss

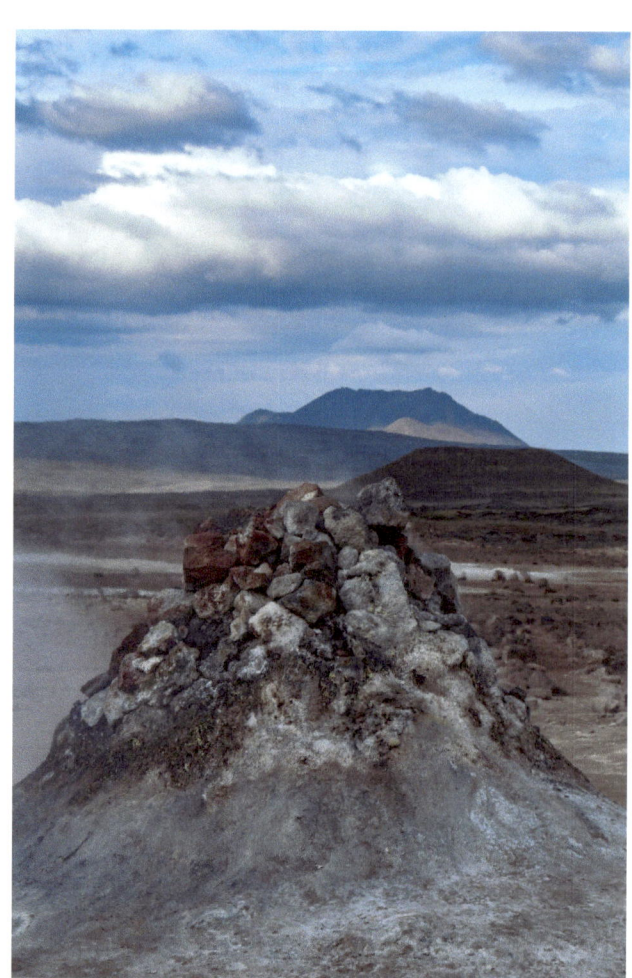

Namafjall Hverir Thermal

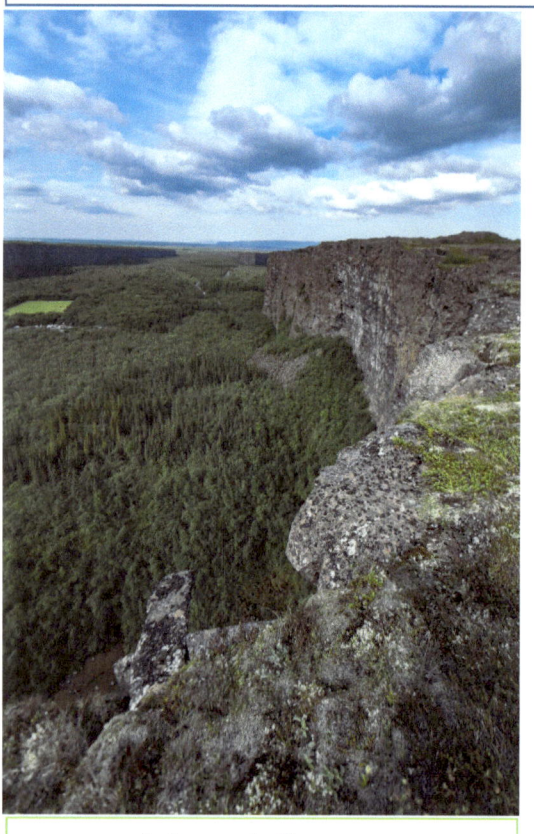

Asbyrtgi Canyon

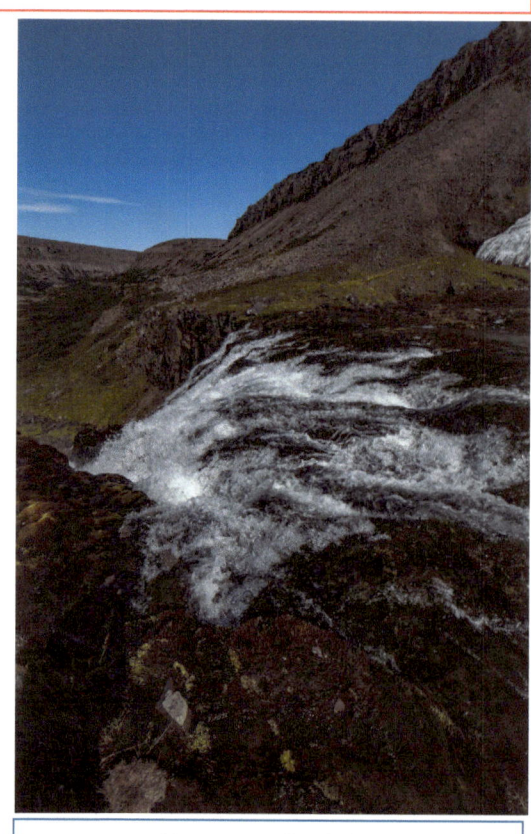

Dynjandi Falls

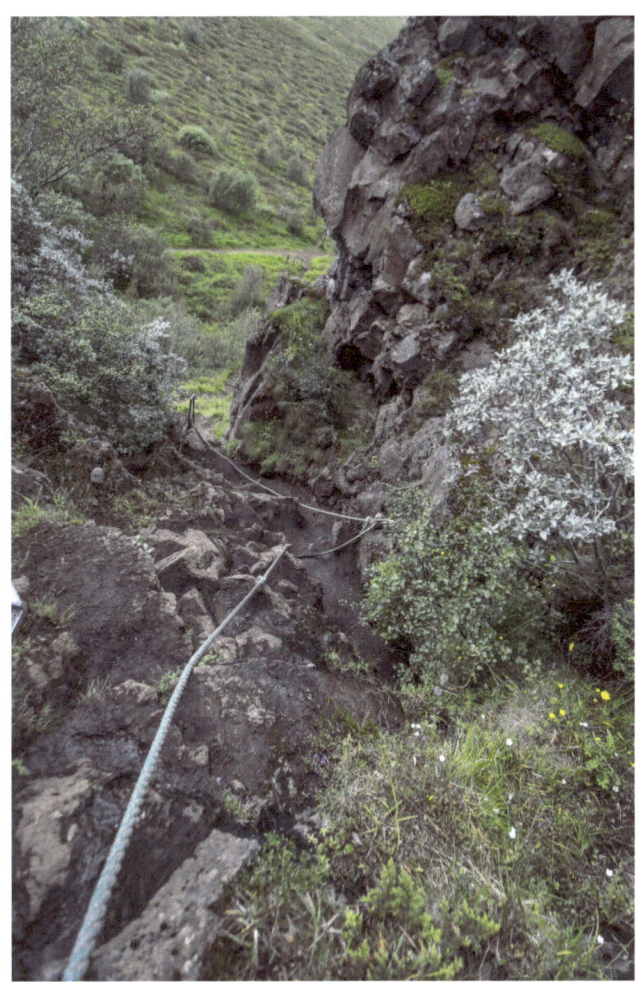

Asbrygi Canyon

At Raidfeldsgja gorge, I climbed up the scree on the right and went as far as I could. I also scaled three waterfalls inside the gorge, with water shoes, in very cold water. The fourth and last one was over 12 feet high. As the adventurers would have it there is of course a frayed worn rope. To climb this would have made you soaking wet in very cold water, so I decided that there was no way. Even some younger kids turned around. I wish I was younger and had climbing gear and just do it. I found my way to B59 hotel in Bogarnes for a beautiful meal at the good restaurant. There was a Polish waitress studying medicine who was in Iceland to make some money for the summer. There was shared room with another very quiet traveler at this well done top notch hotel.

I did the small lower West Fjord hike to Kirkjufell and Raudfeldsgja gorge on one of the last days. I met more tourists, but also got off trail and waded in the water, and crossed in a couple feet with bare feet. By law I can not travel on F-roads which are 4x4 roads, but in planning for this section the night before, Google maps had showed me on one. I had wifi every night in various accomodations but never had a calling plan. Up to the glacier at Snaefellsjokullit proved way too much for my sedan car. I seriously enjoyed the approach to the valley, as it was this beautiful never ending decent into a long beach near Raudfeldsgja gorge off the mountain.

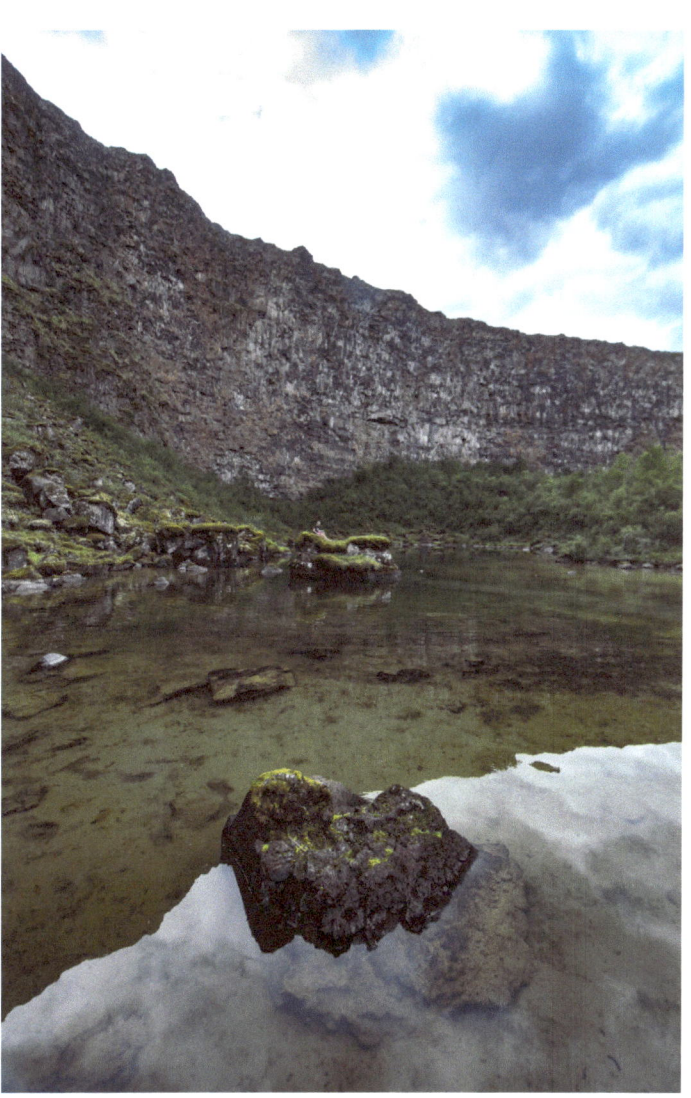

Asbrygi Canyon

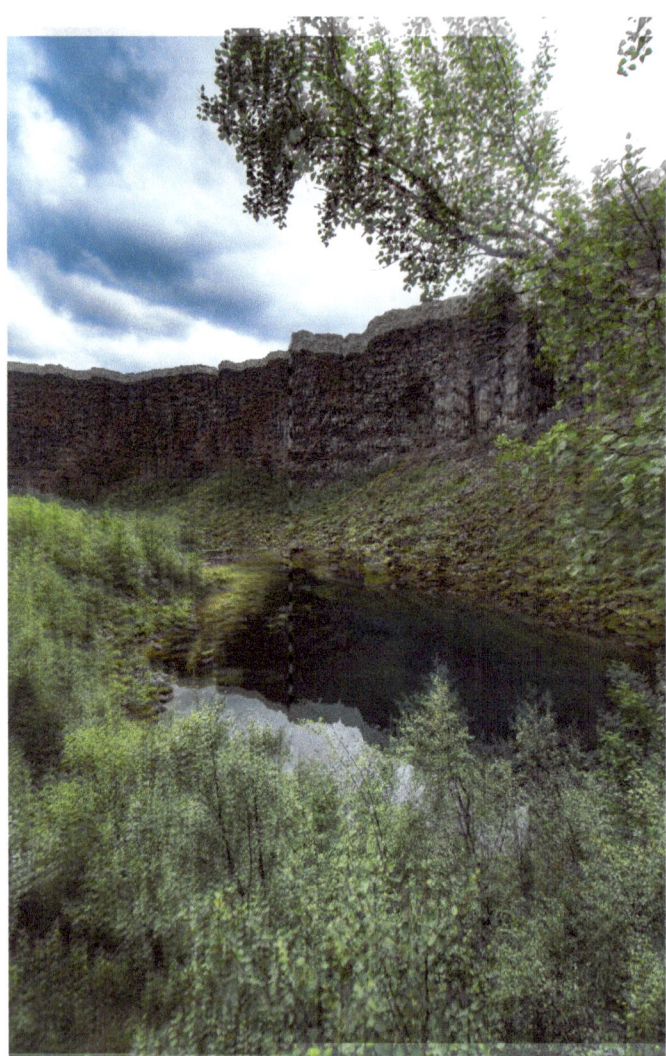

Asbrygi Canyon

The next day I went to Glymur falls and took a loop hike of maybe 5 miles round trip as the very last hiking destination. I drove to Barnafoss and Hraunfossar for the short visit at these tourist falls, and found some information about Vigelmir cave and snowmobile tours in the area. I drove into Reykjavik for 2 hours and found the art museum, a flea market, and some culture but never really found my stride in town with time limited for a flight home. When I got home a had a speeding ticket in the mail. Oh well, I guess I wont be going back, I had a wonderful time.

> Our happiest moments always seem to come when we stumble upon one thing while in pursuit of another. – Lawrence Block
>
> Stuff your eyes with wonder, live as if you'd drop dead in a second. The world is more fantastic than anything made – Ray Bradbury

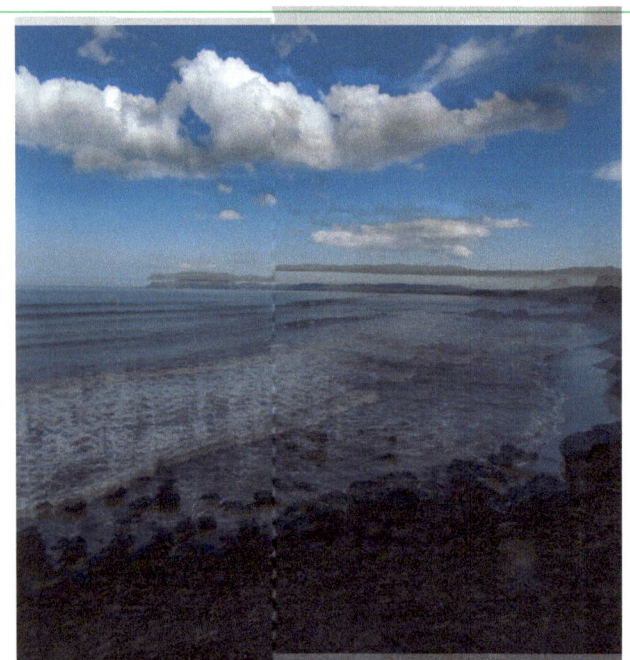

Endless Seas

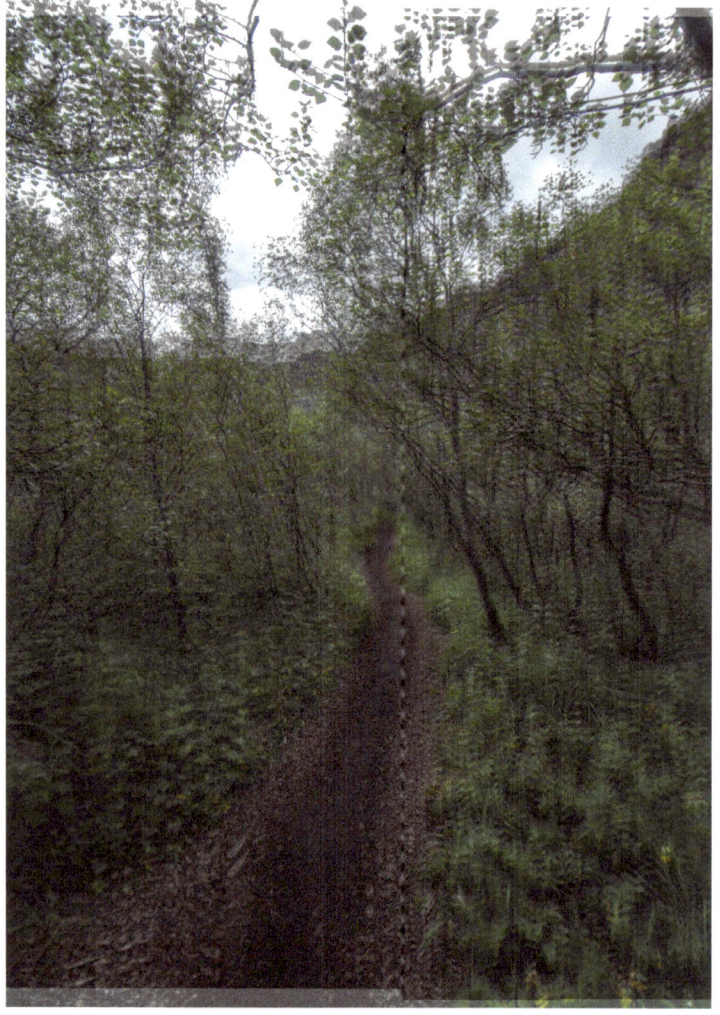

Asbrygi Canyon

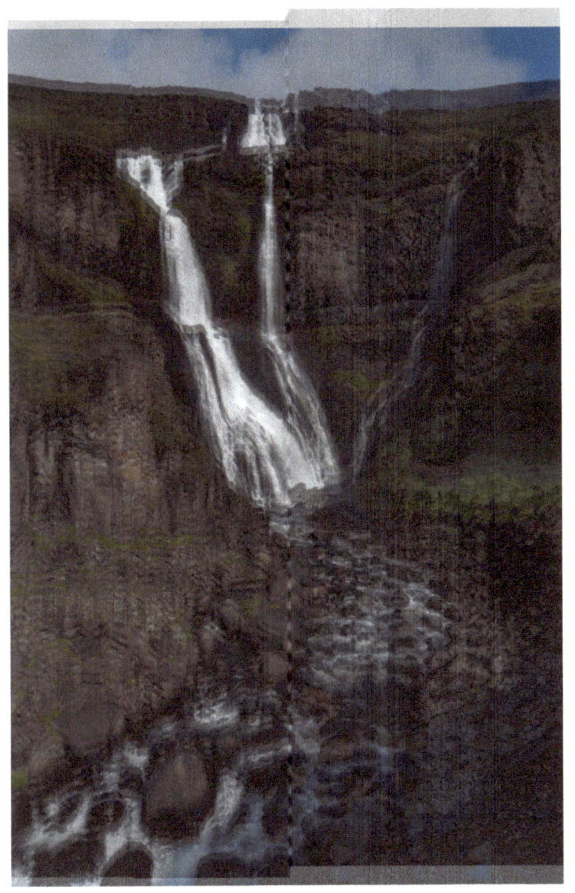

Skogafoss Canyon

There is so much more to life than work. It is great to be passionate about something, and the world moves because of "ideas plus action," but one of the glaring differences between many of the places I have visited and the U.S. is that people take the other pillars of their lives just as, if not more, seriously than their jobs.

Traveling has taught me that there is no higher compliment than showing interest in someone and truly listening to what they have to say. No greater joy than discovery of something you have never seen. After all, the best memories and greatest lessons are often not seen, but heard, and experienced. Our parents don't see us as we are, but they see the kids they remember. Our friends don't see us as we are, but they see the friend they remember. Only a stranger met on your travels sees you as you truly are right now.

> All journeys have secret destinations of which the traveller is unaware. – *Martin Buber*
>
> All that is gold does not glitter; just as not all those who wander are lost. – *JRR Tolkien*
>
> Travel makes a wise man better; and a fool worse. – *Thomas Fuller*
>
> Great things are done when men and mountains meet. – *William Blake*

The beauty of traveling is that we each come away with something different. It opens your eyes to the reality of the person I had become and gave me a glimpse of the person I was capable of being. In short, traveling taught me to bet on myself again, and keep the dream alive.

Fail forward, and survive the change of winds direction; nothing in travel is ever perfect and in that lies its beauty. We stumble forward and fail often. As a reward, traveling takes us to the places we were always meant to go, and in the process teaches us about who we were always meant to be. We find inner peace, meaning, and reflection upon what we do, what we see, and whom we impact and cure and heal ourselves to be better.

Comparisons steal joy; be yourself and do what moves you.

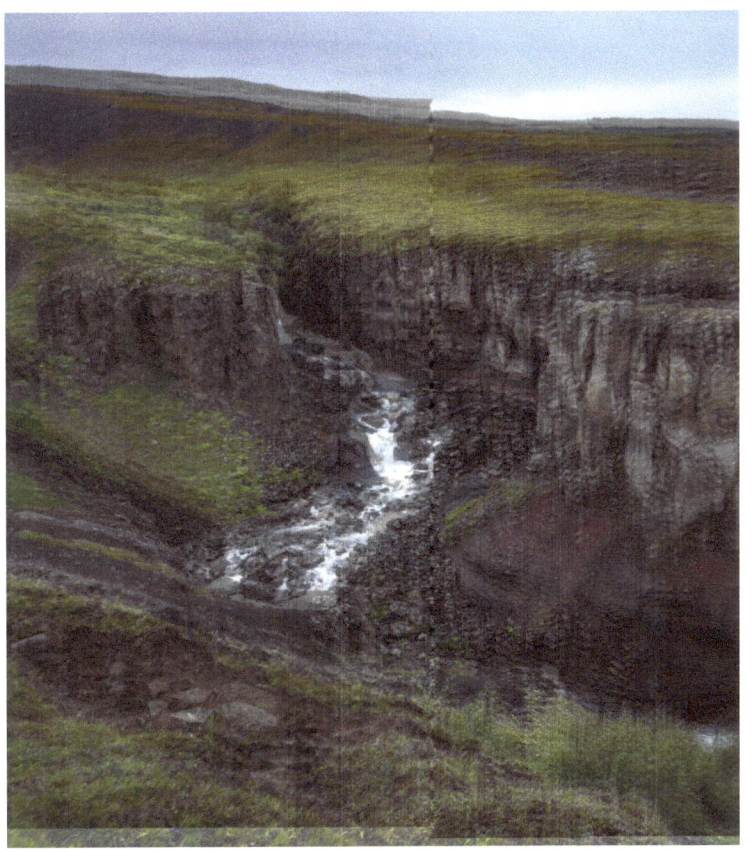

Skogafoss Canyon

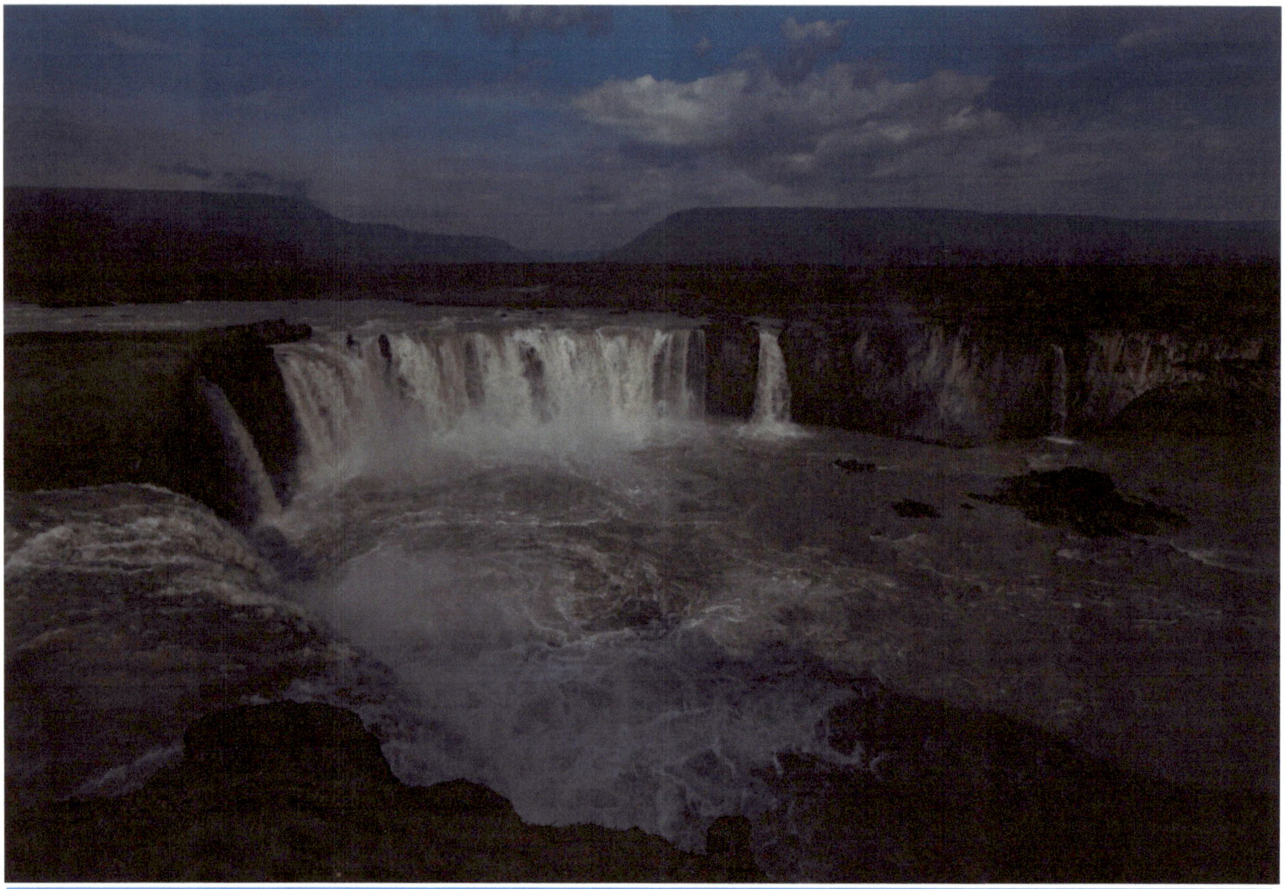

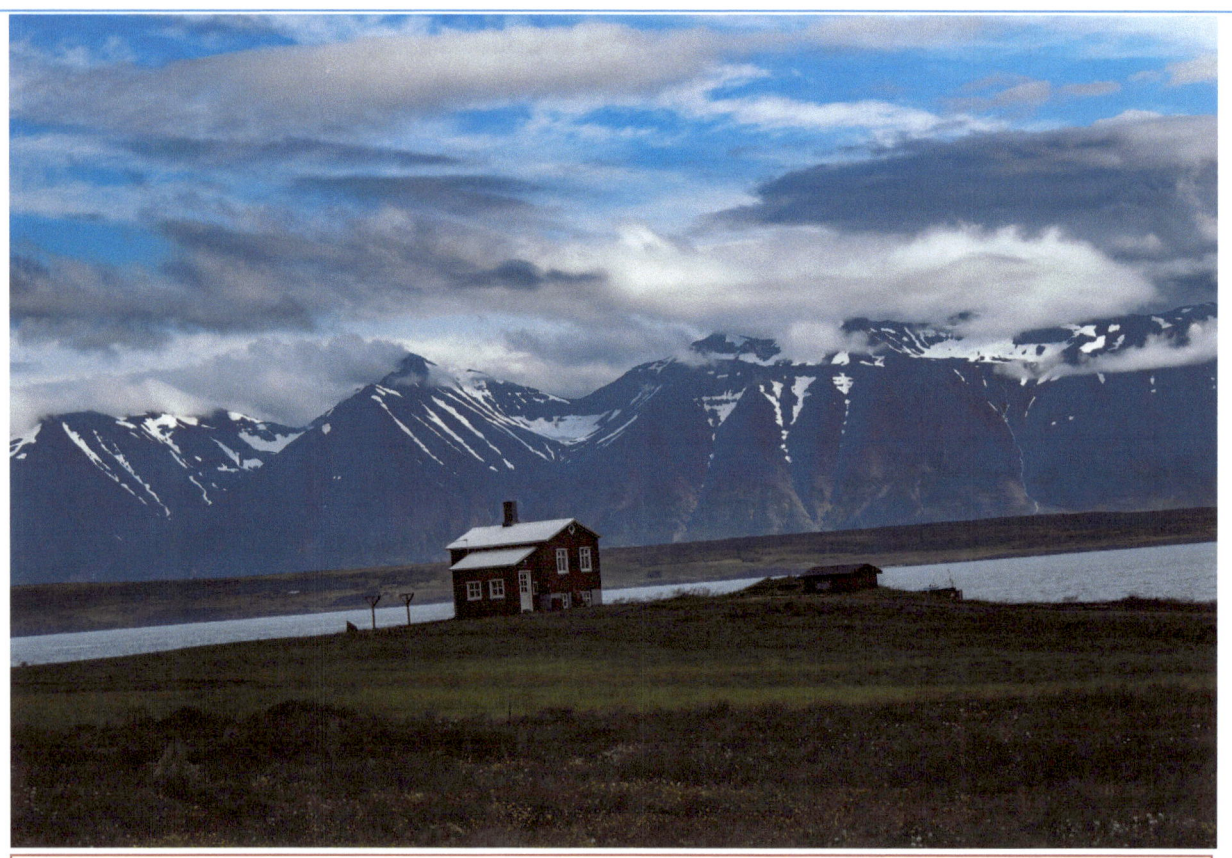

Dettifoss Falls

Drive up North from Ayureyri

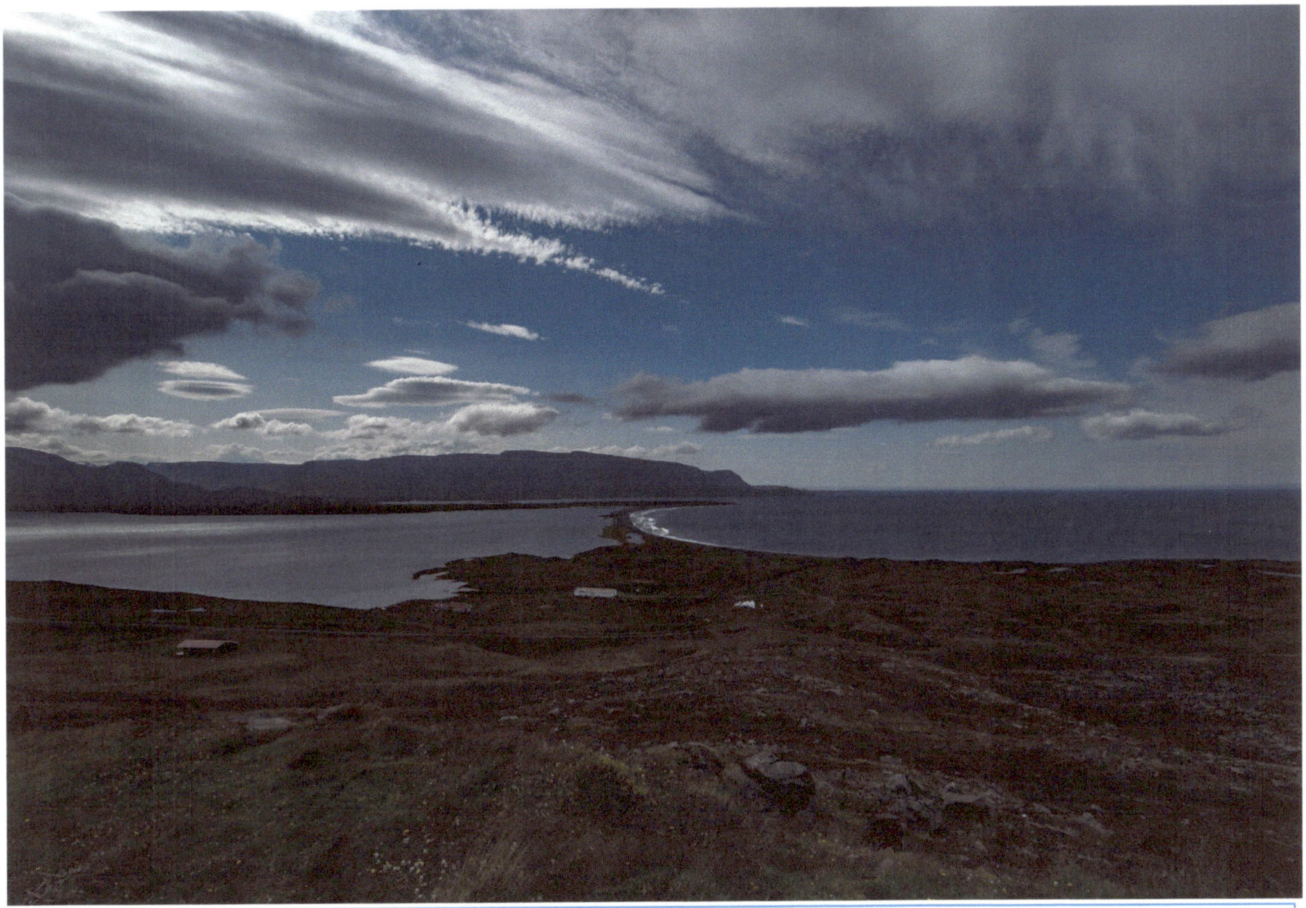

Endless Skies and Land Bridges

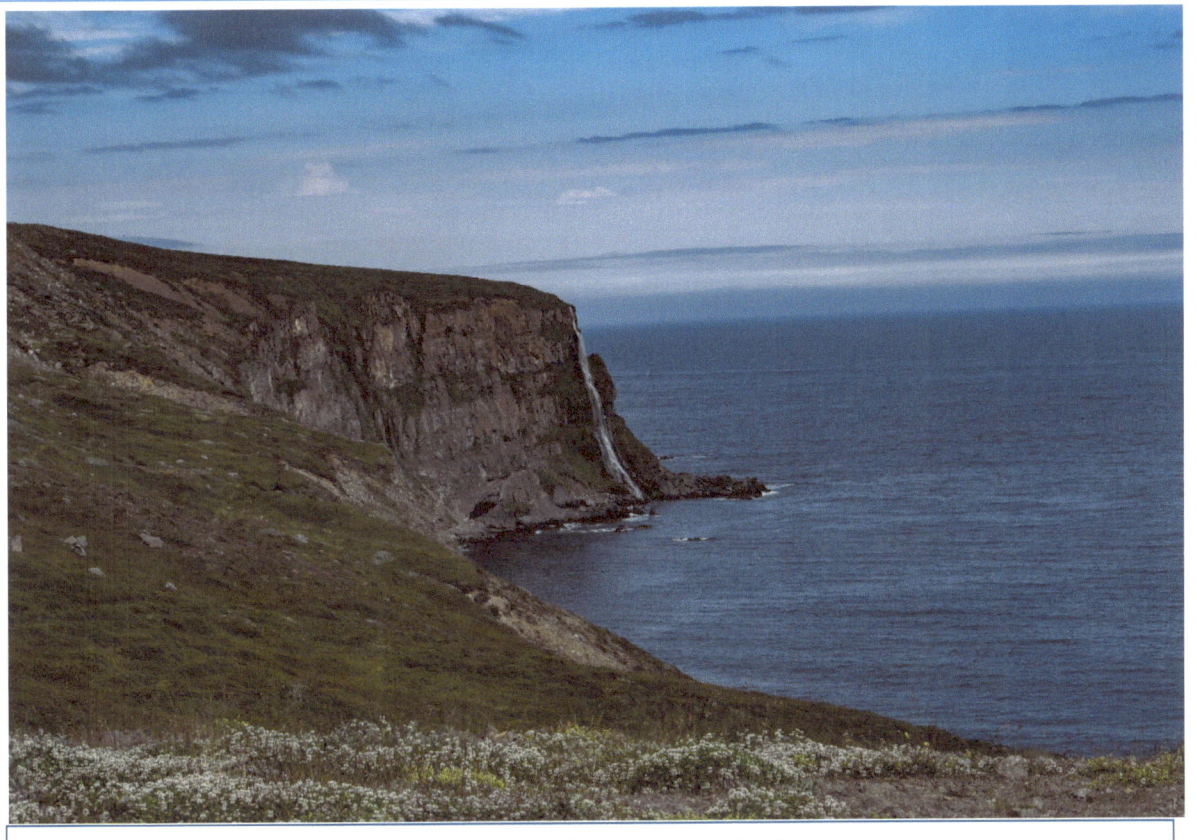

Falls Into The North Sea

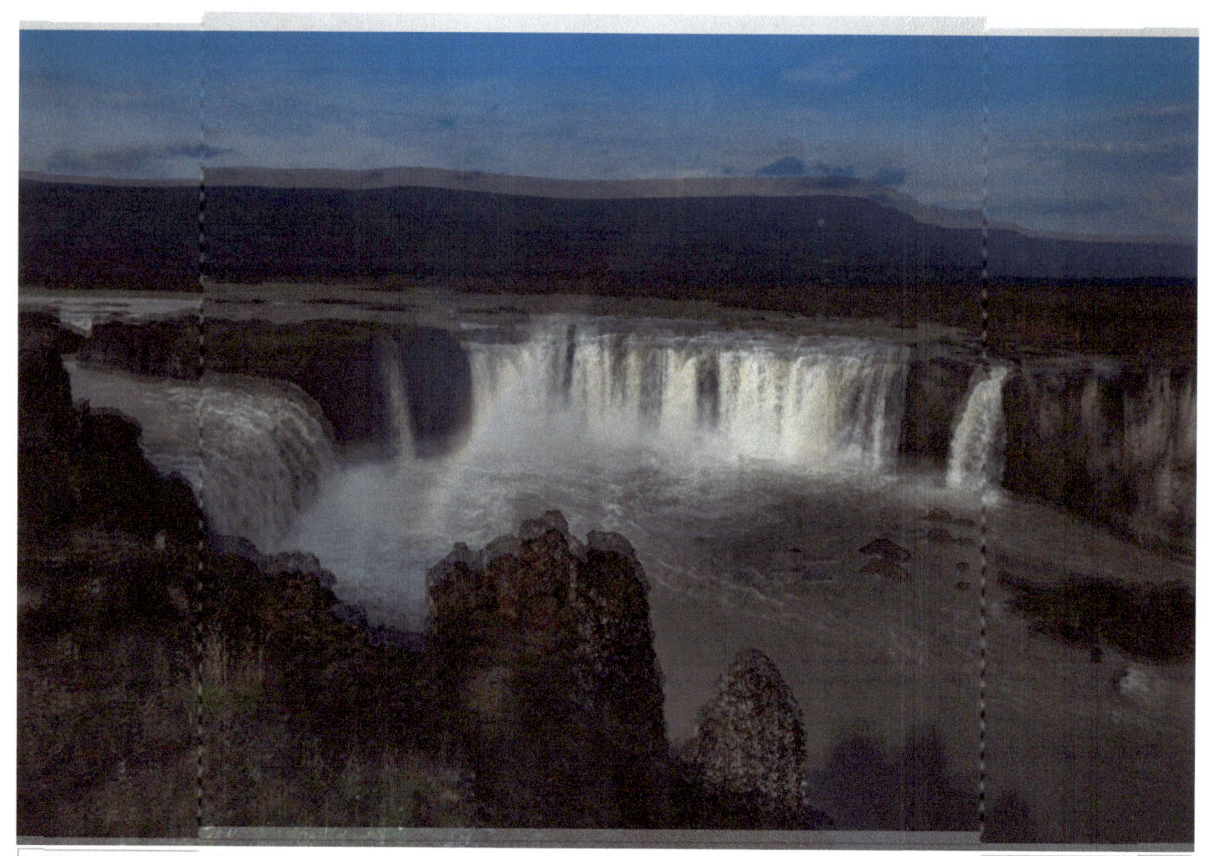

Dettifoss Falls

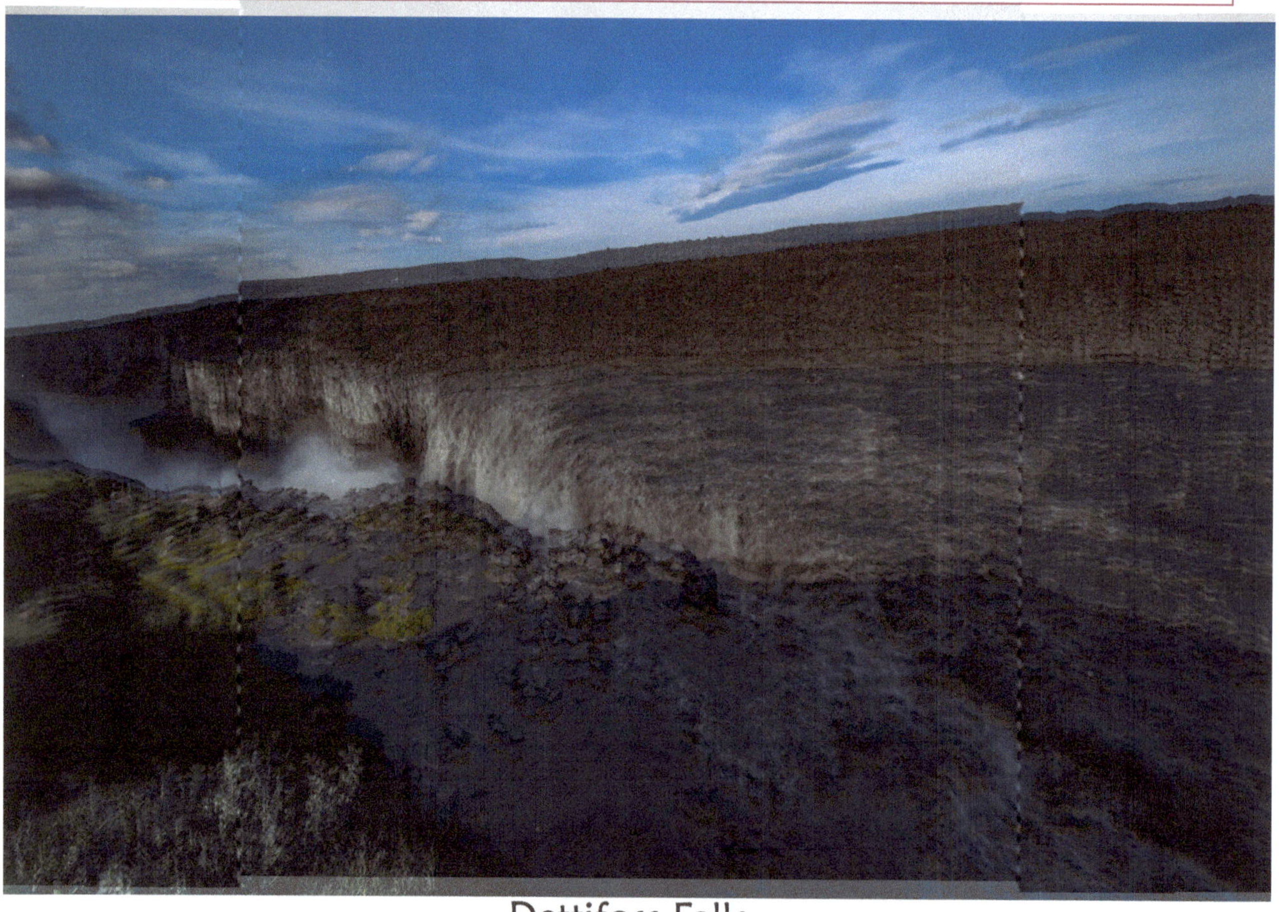

Dettifoss Falls

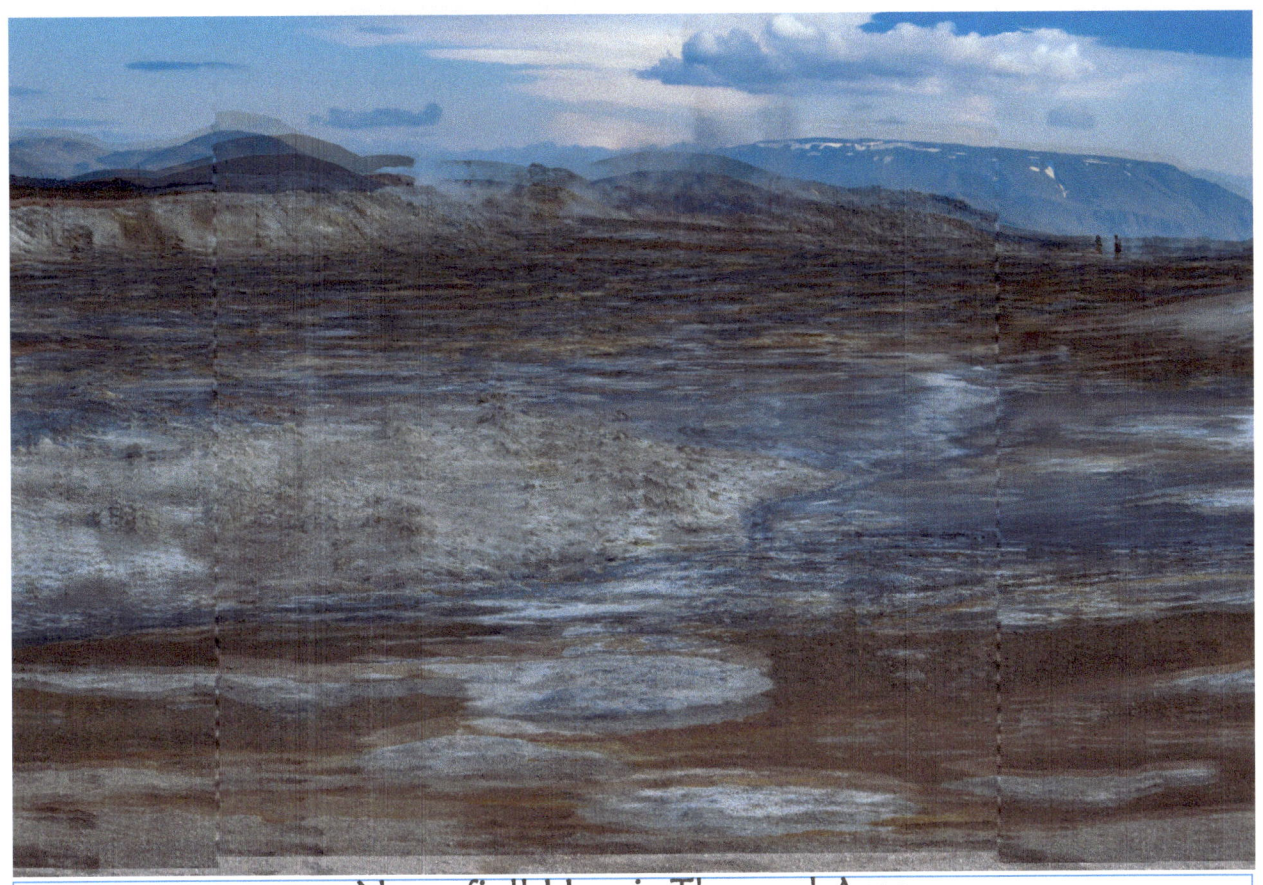
Namafjall Hverir Thermal Area

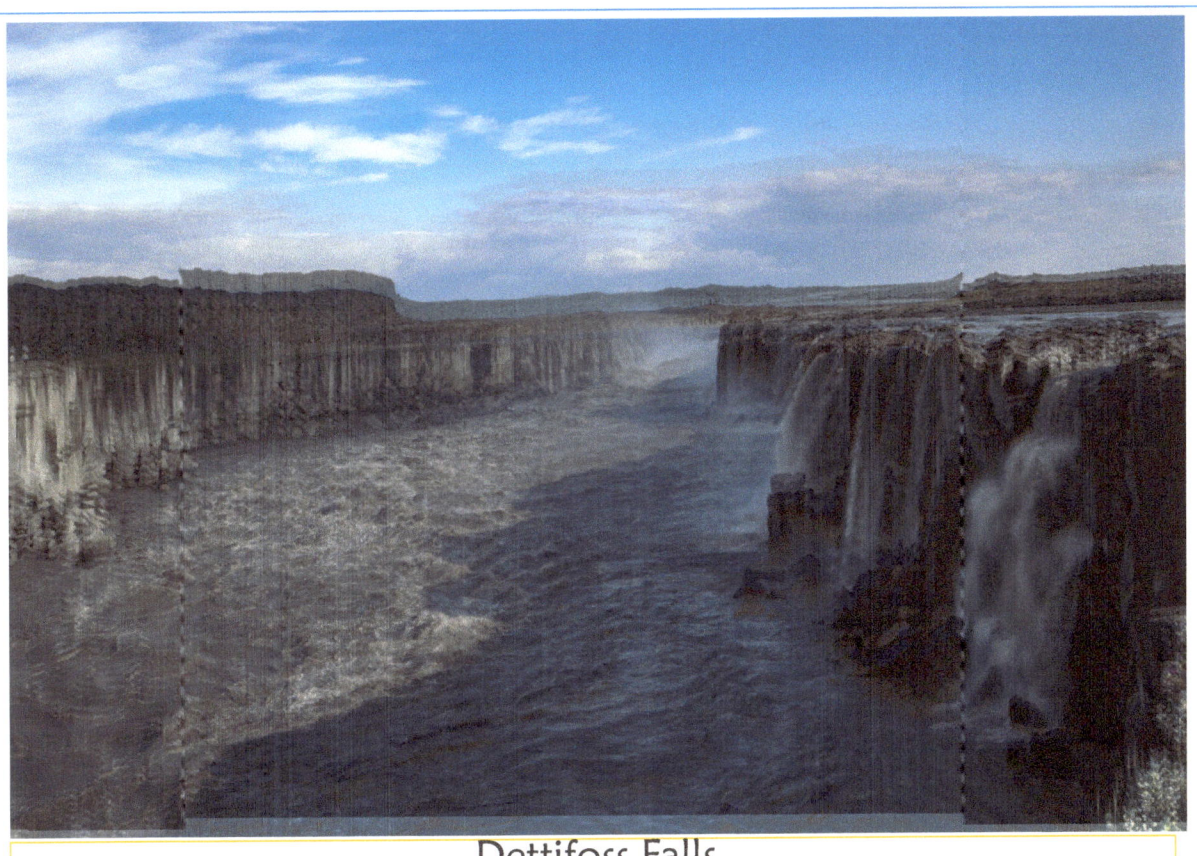
Dettifoss Falls

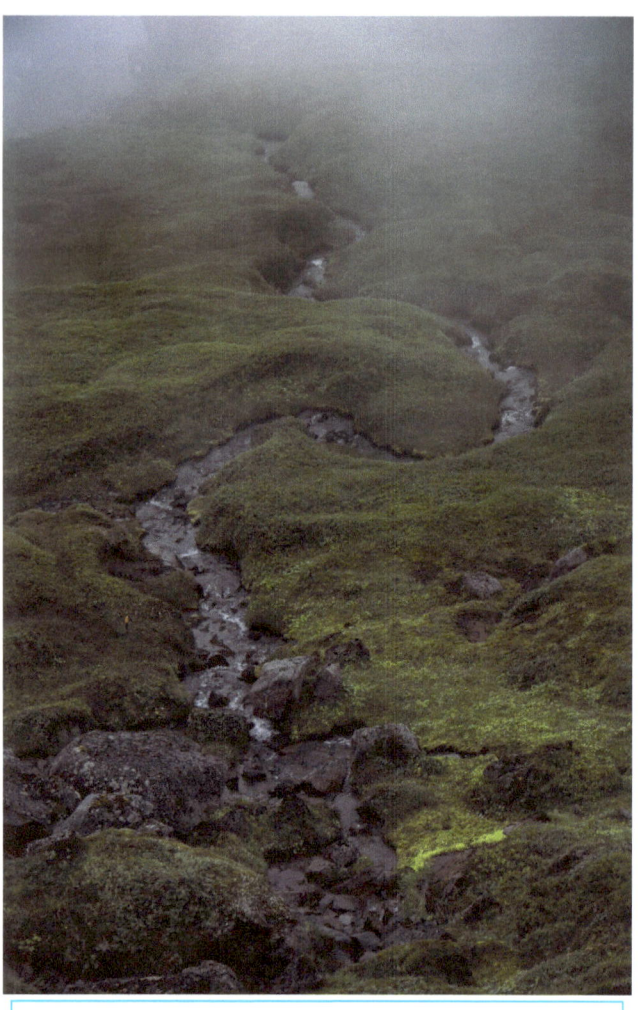

Streams Through The Fog

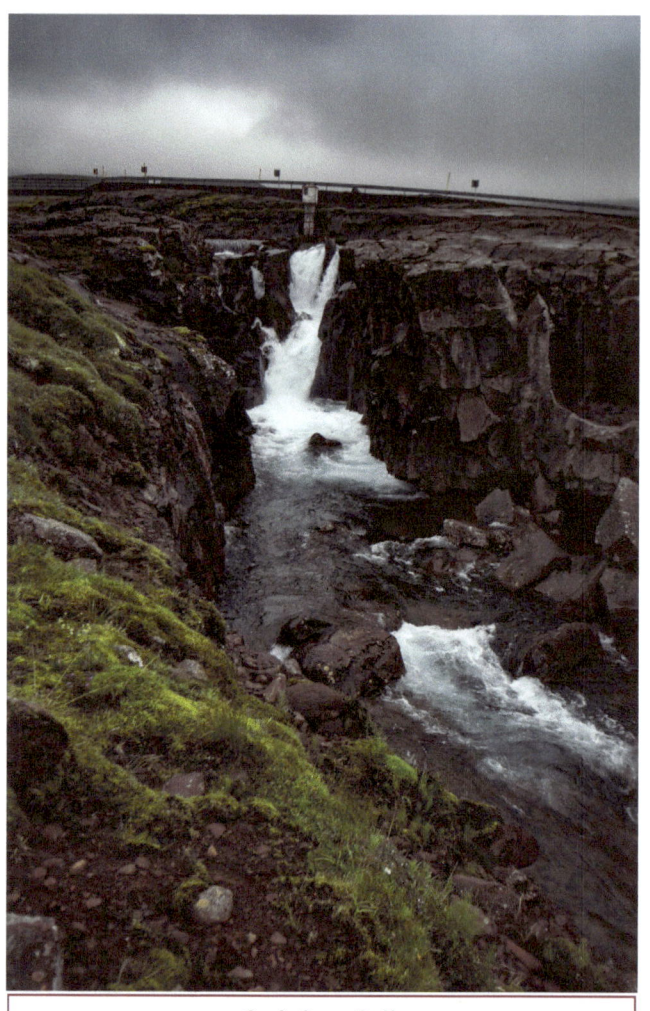

Gufufoss Falls

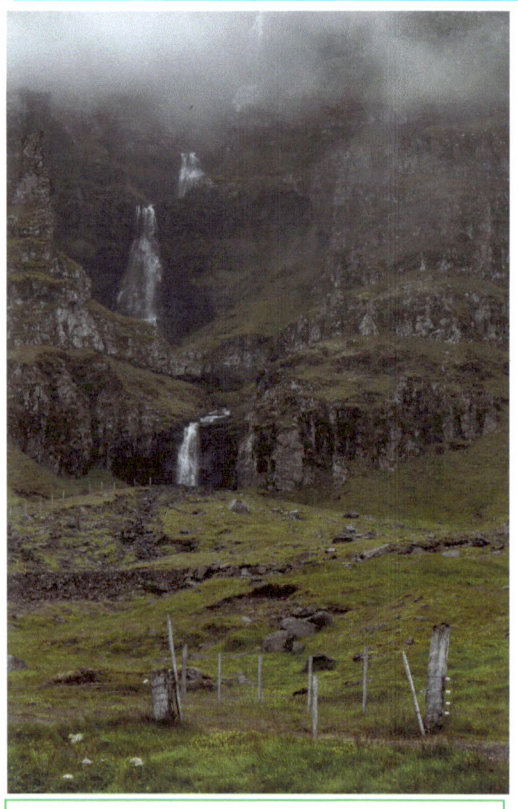

Endless Falls Into The Fog

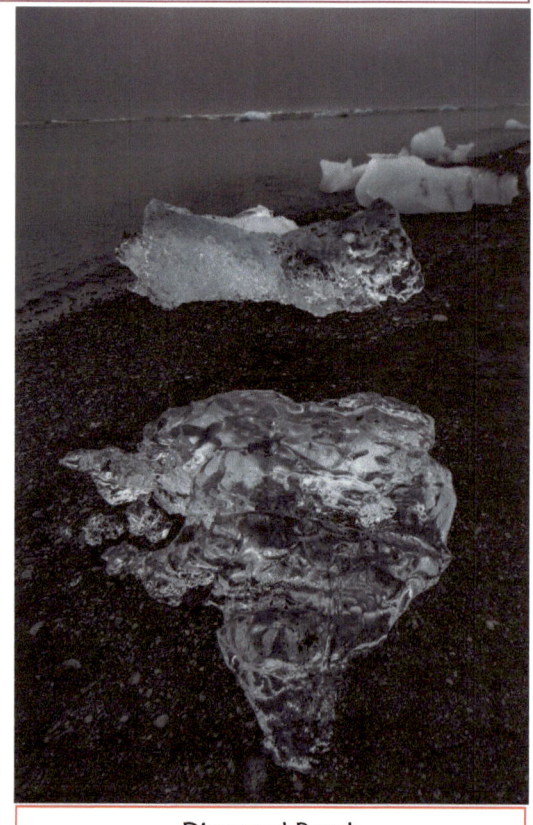

Diamond Beach

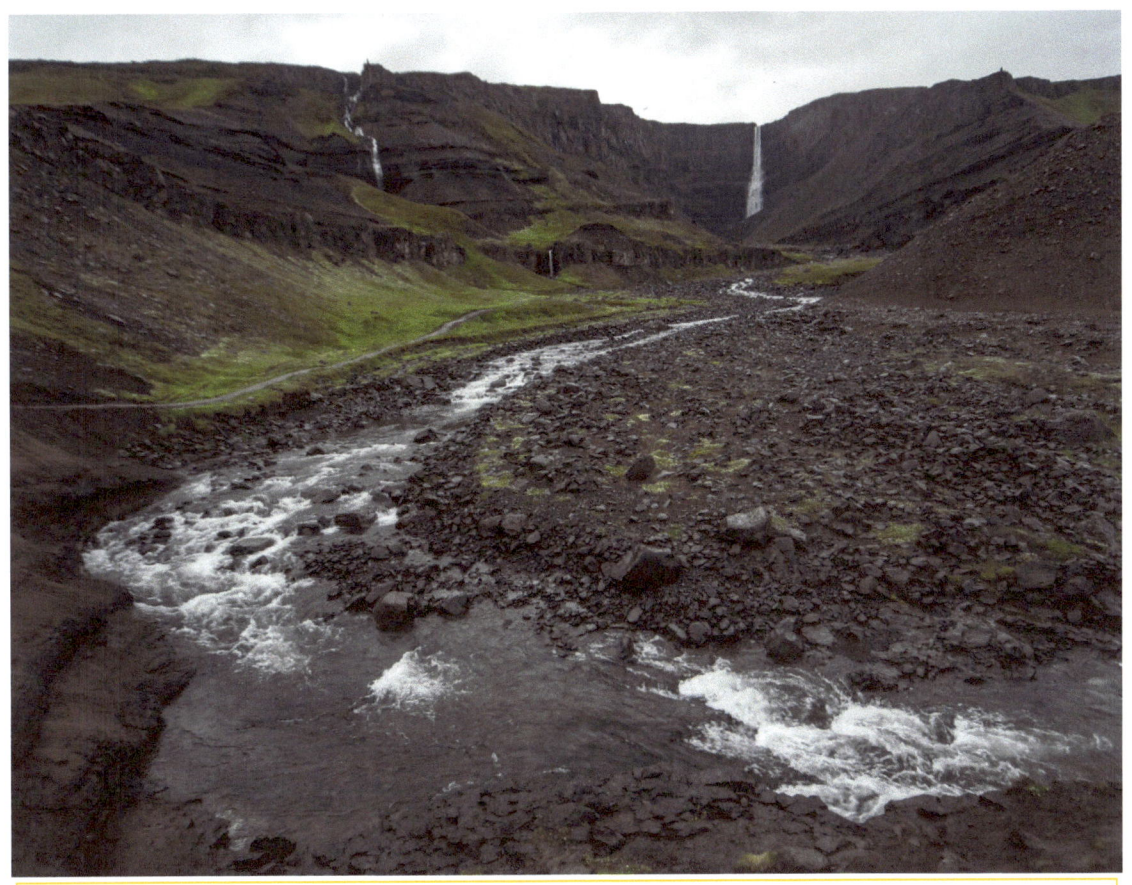

Svartifoss Falls

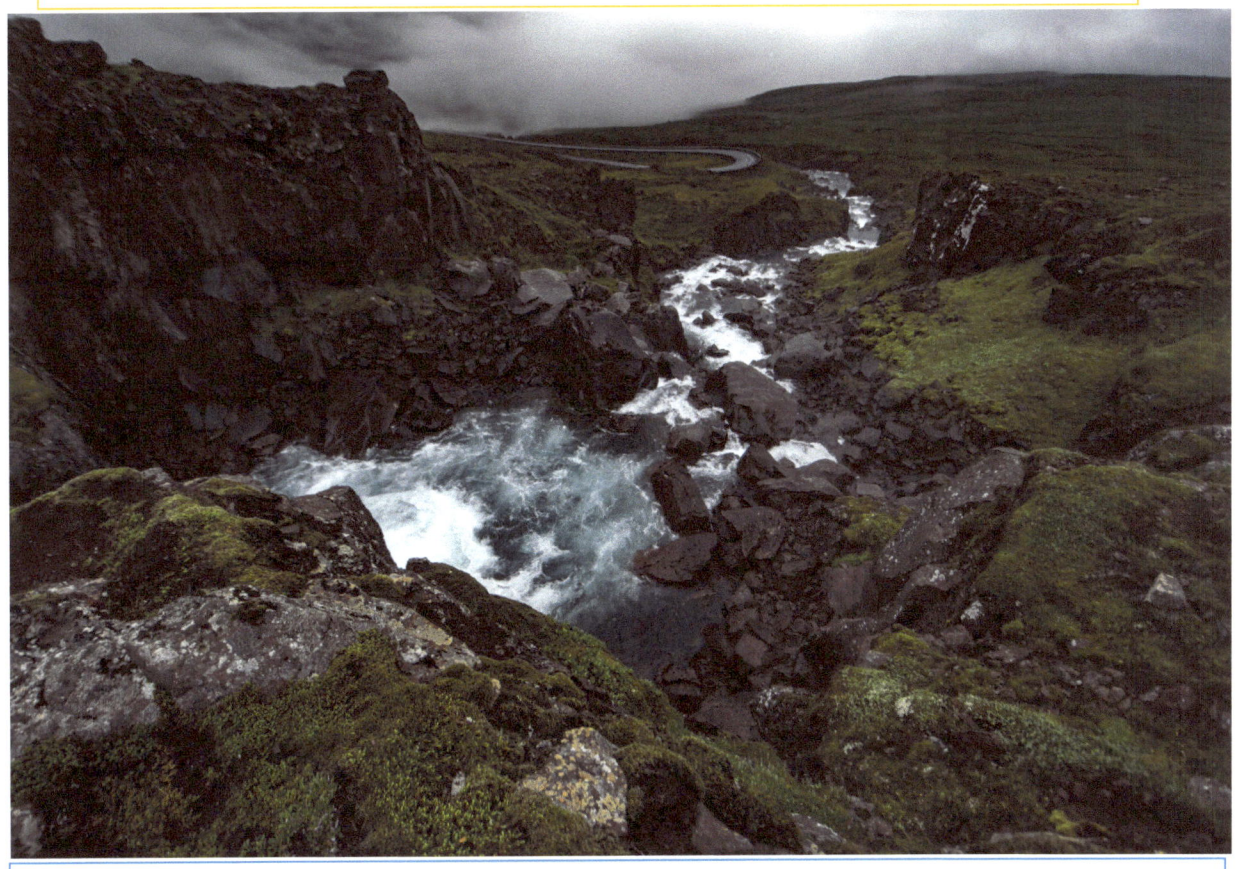

Gufufoss Falls

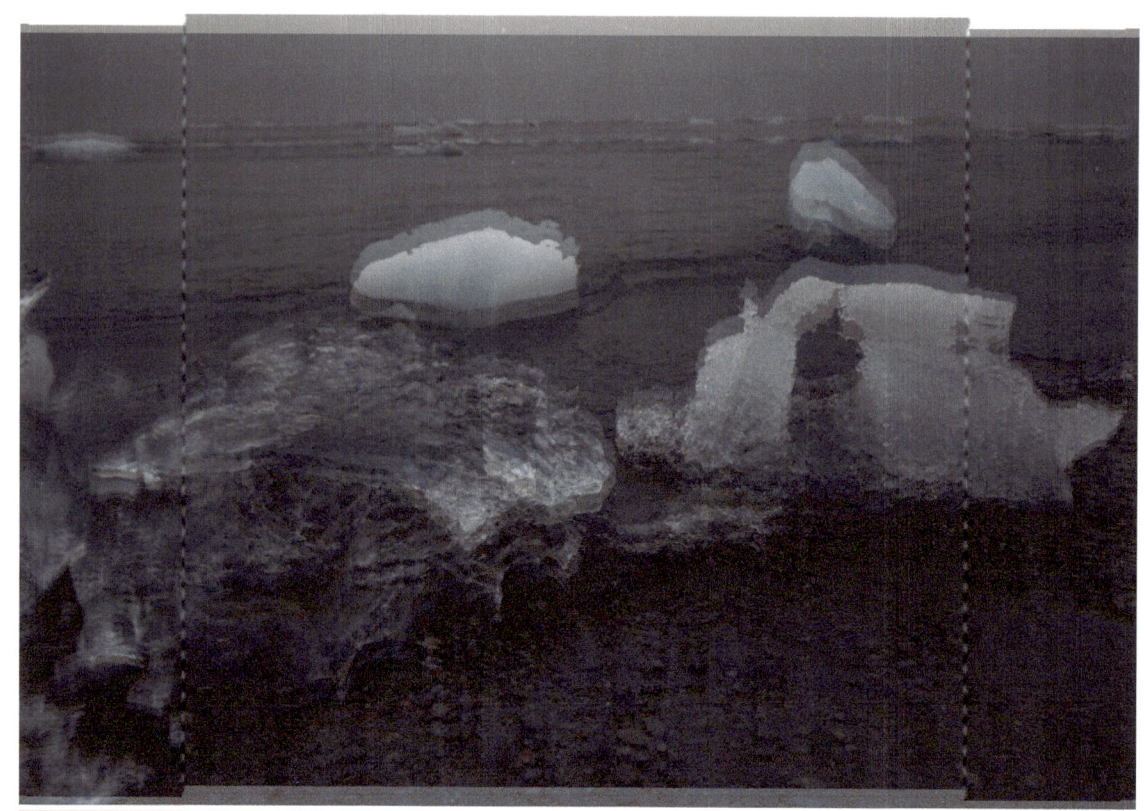

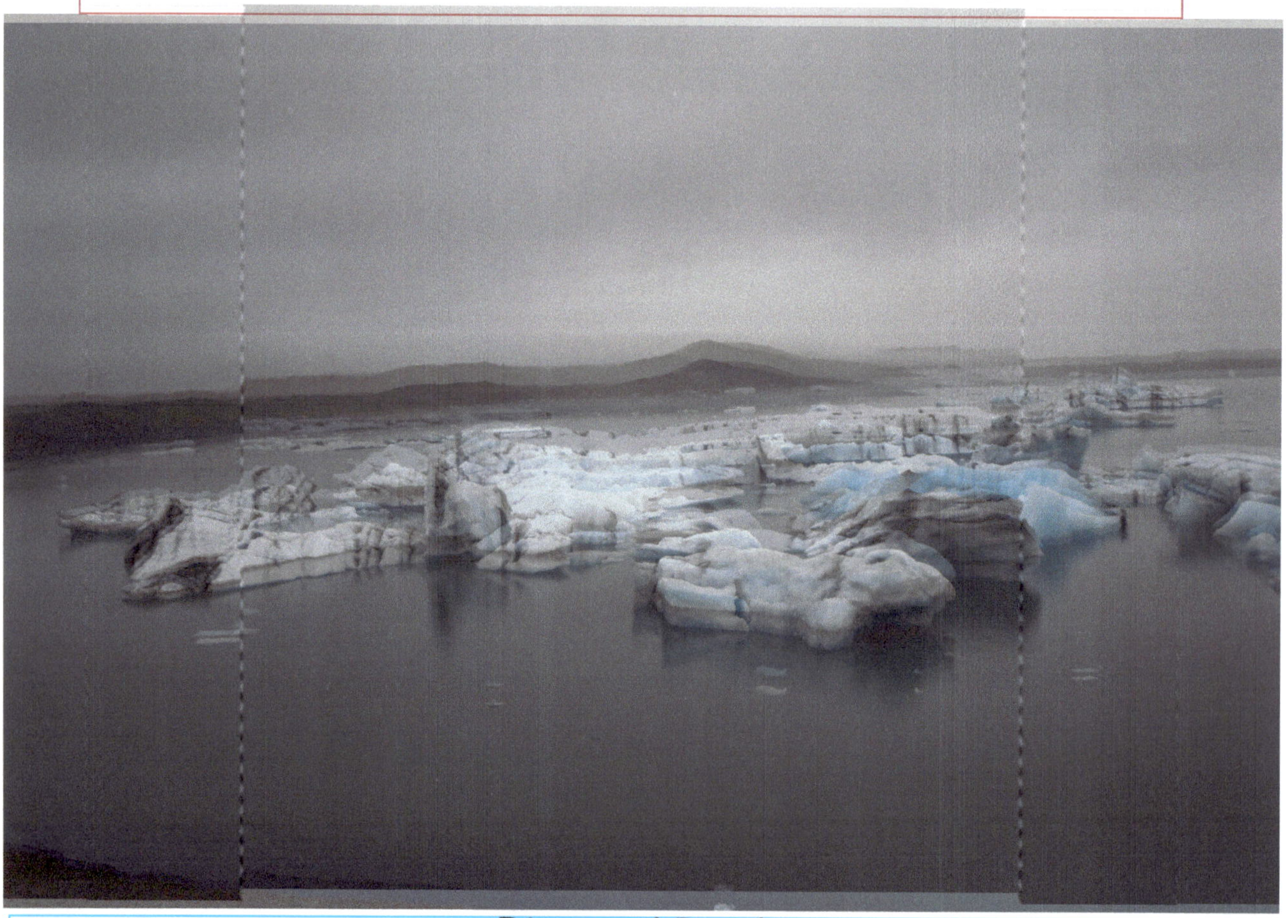

Diamond Beach

Diamond Beach

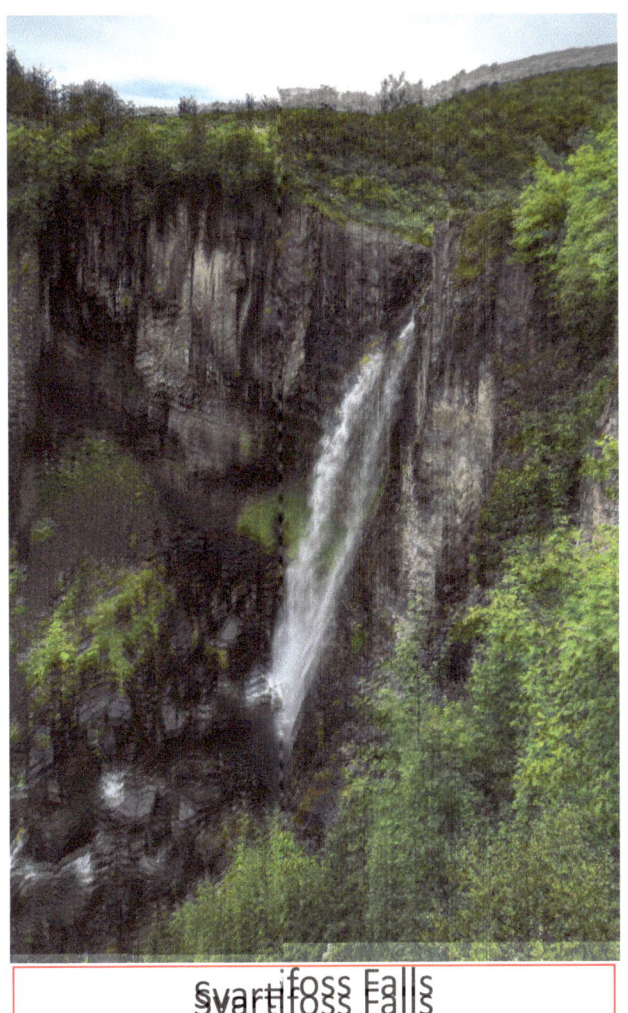

Svartifoss Falls

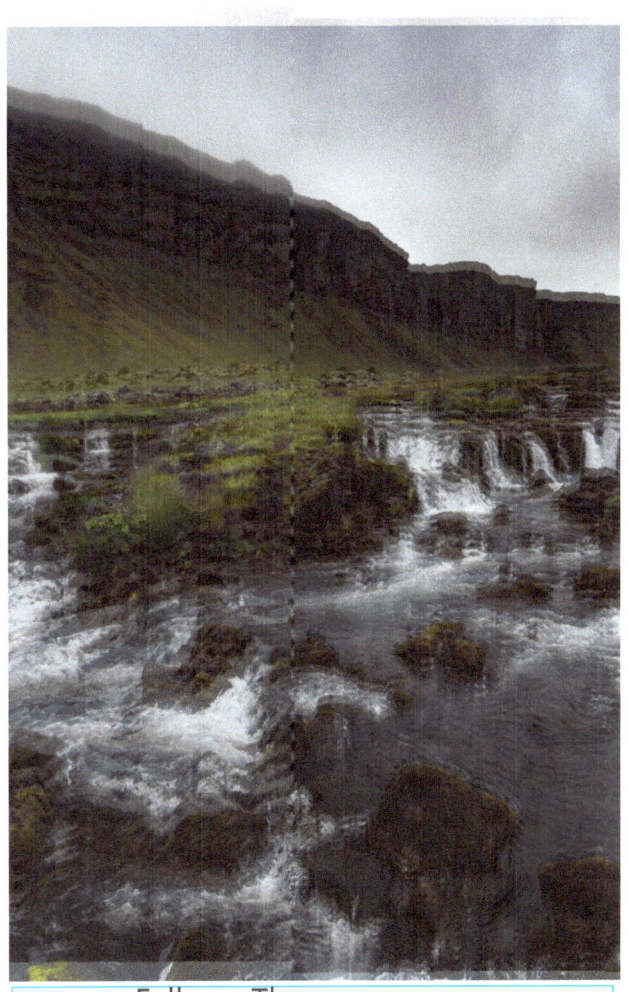

Falls on The South Shore

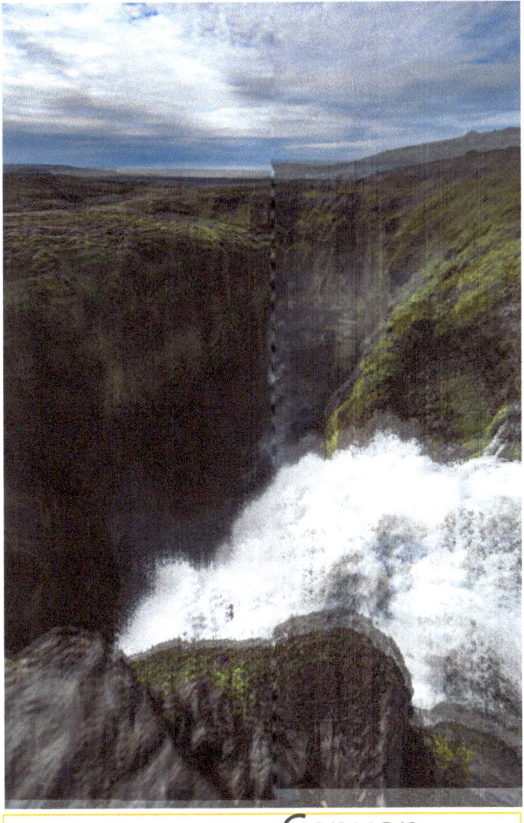

Skogafoss Canyon

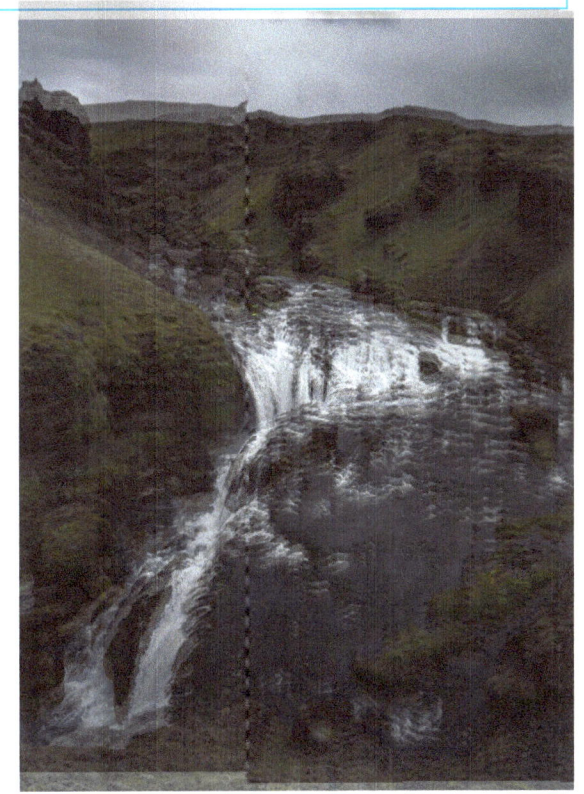

Skogafoss Canyon

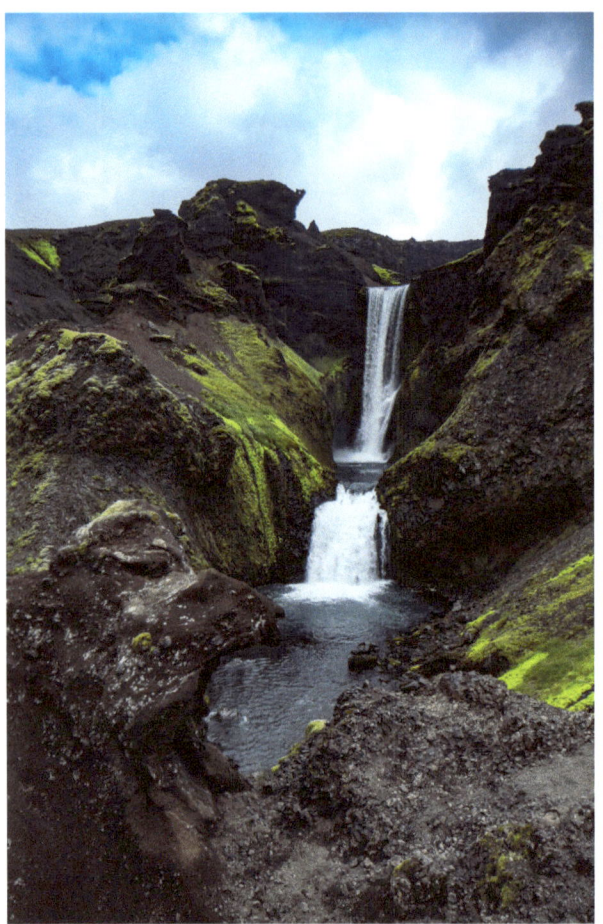

Skogafoss Canyon

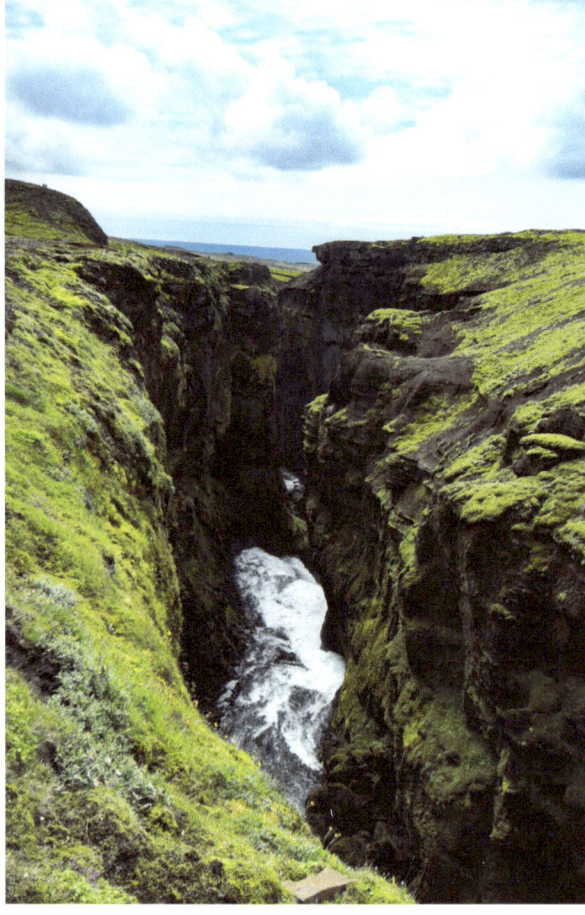

Skogafoss Canyon

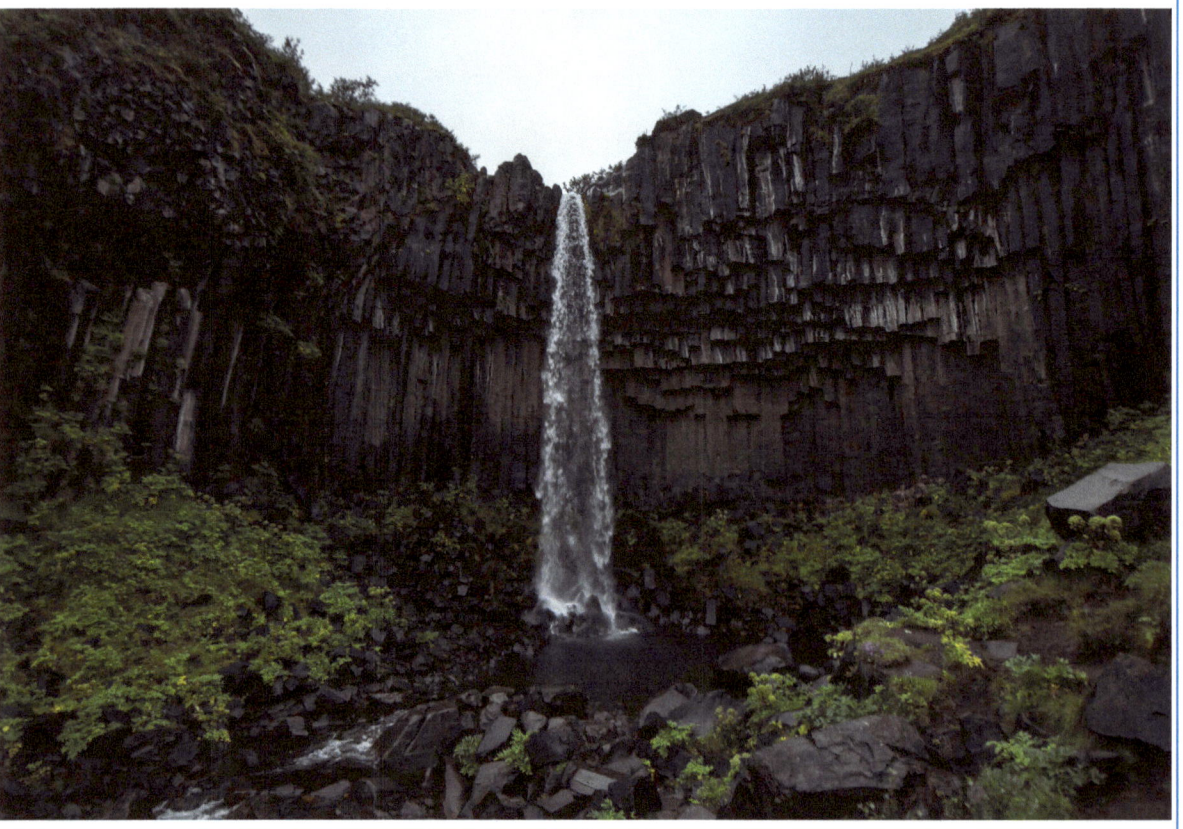

Svartifoss Falls

Travel is fatal to prejudice, bigotry, and narrow mindedness., and many of our people need it sorely on these accounts.— Mark Twain

The real voyage of discovery consists not in seeking new landscapes, but in having new eyes. — Marcel Proust

If you think adventure is dangerous, try routine, it's lethal.

Great things never came from comfort zones. If you are always trying to be normal, you will never know how amazing you can be. Stop worrying about the potholes in the road and enjoy the journey. Fear is only temporary. Regrets last forever. Without new experiences, something inside of us sleeps. The sleeper must awaken." – Frank Herbert

The use of traveling is to regulate imagination by reality, and instead of thinking how things may be, to see them as they are. – Samuel Johnson

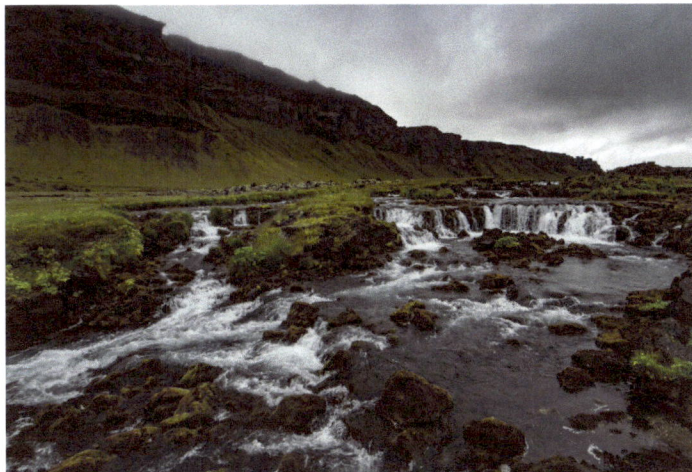
Falls off The Road On The South Shore Of Iceland

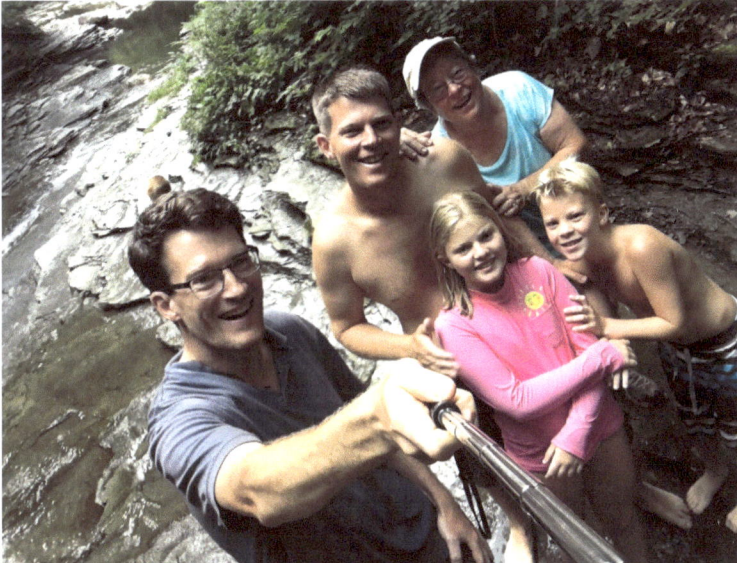
A hike in Chautauqua with family.

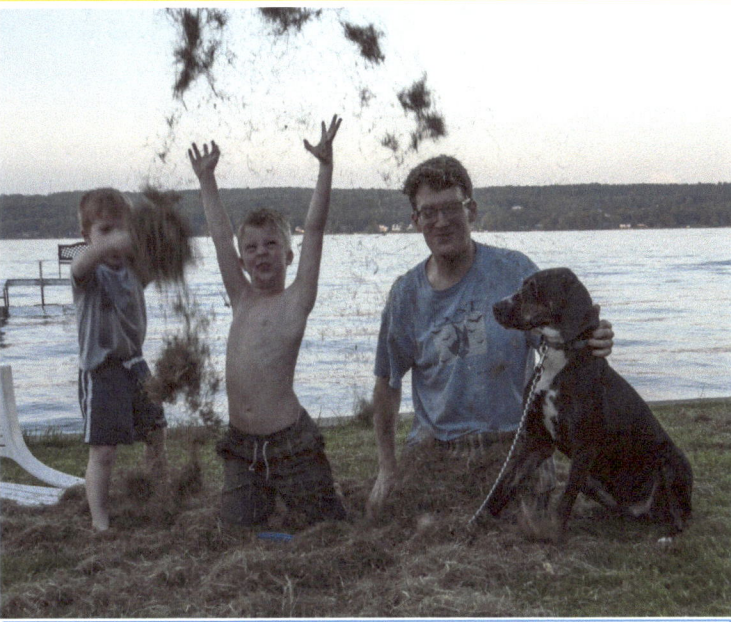
A joyful moment in time.

He who bends himself to joy, does the winged life destroy. but he who kisses the joy as it flies, lives in eternity's sunrise." William Blake

Be thankful for what you have; you'll end up having more. If you concentrate on what you don't have, you will never, ever have enough. -- Oprah Winfrey

Character cannot be developed in ease and quiet. Only through experience of trial and suffering can the soul be strengthened, ambition inspired, and success achieved.
-- Helen Keller
Dream lofty dreams, and as you dream, so you shall become. Your vision is the promise of what you shall one day be; your ideal is the prophecy of what you shall at last unveil.
-- James Allen
Even if I don't reach all my goals, I've gone higher than I would have if I hadn't set any.
-- Danielle Fotopoulis
Failure should be our teacher, not our undertaker. Failure is delay, not defeat. It is a temporary detour, not a dead end. Failure is something we can avoid only by saying nothing, doing nothing, and being nothing.
-- Denis Waitley
Feeling grateful or appreciative of someone or something in your life actually attracts more of the things that you appreciate and value into your life.
-- Christiane Northrup
Finish each day and be done with it. You have done what you could. Some blunders and absurdities no doubt crept in; forget them as soon as you can. Tomorrow is a new day; begin it well and serenely and with too high a spirit to be encumbered with your old nonsense.
-- Ralph Waldo Emerson
I am only one, but still I am one. I cannot do everything, but still I can do something; and because I cannot do everything, I will not refuse to do something that I can do.
-- Helen Keller
I expect to pass through this world but once. Any good, therefore, that I can do or any kindness I can show to any fellow creature, let me do it now. Let me not defer or neglect it for I shall not pass this way again.
-- Stephen Grellet
If everything is smooth sailing right from the beginning, we cannot become people of substance and character. By surmounting paining setbacks and obstacles, we can create a brilliant history of triumph that will shine forever. That is what makes life so exciting and enjoyable. In any field of endeavour, those who overcome hardships and grow as human beings are advancing towards success and victory in life.
-- Daisaku Ikeda
If one advances confidently in the direction of one's dreams, and endeavors to live the life which one has imagined, one will meet with a success unexpected in common hours.
-- Henry David Thoreau
In the depth of winter, I finally learned that within me there lay an invincible summer.
-- Albert Camus
It is one of the most beautiful compensations of life, that no man can sincerely try to help another without helping himself. -- Ralph Waldo
If you wish to travel far and fast, travel light. Take off all your envies, jealousies, unforgiveness, selfishness and fears. –
Cesare Paves

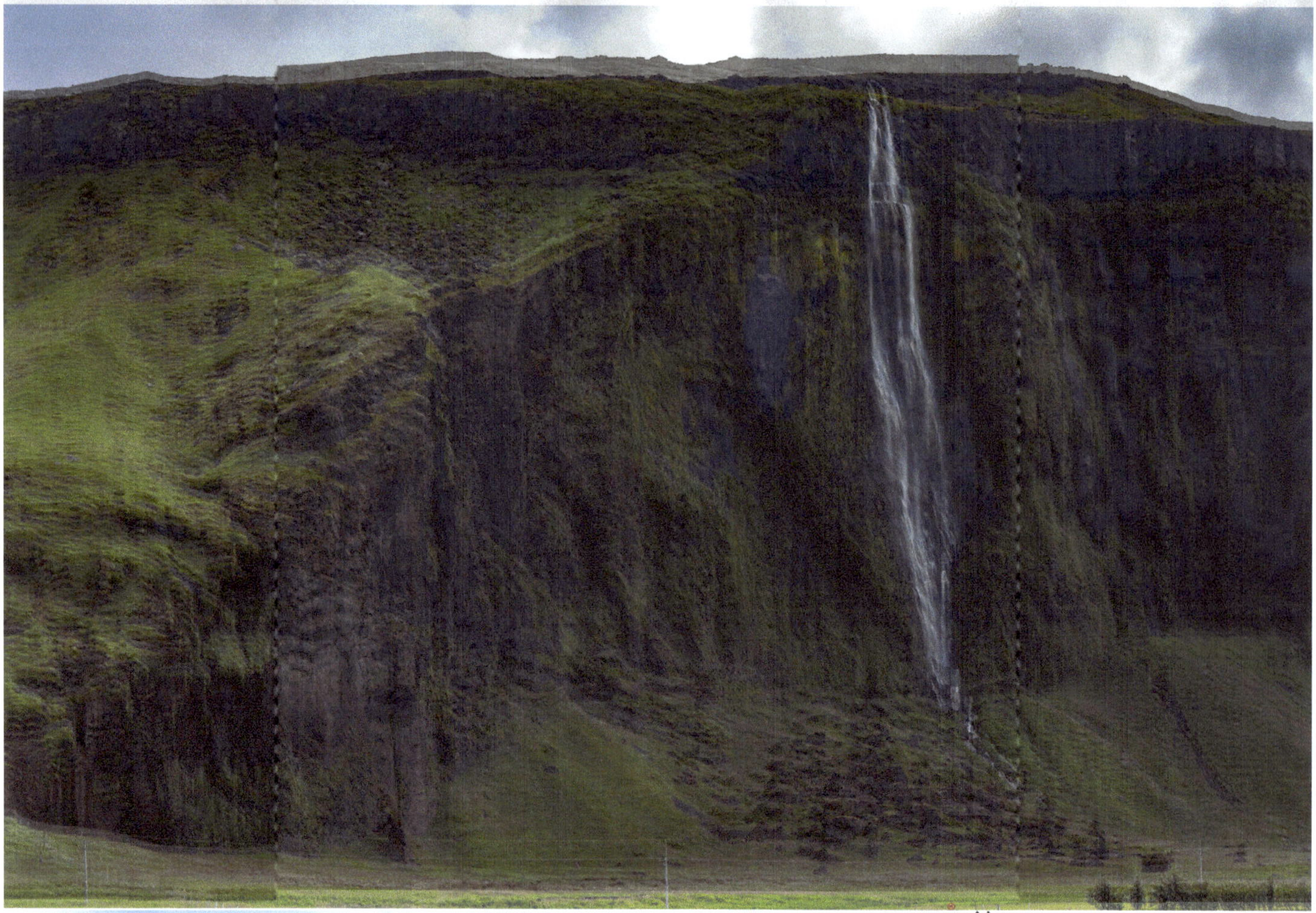

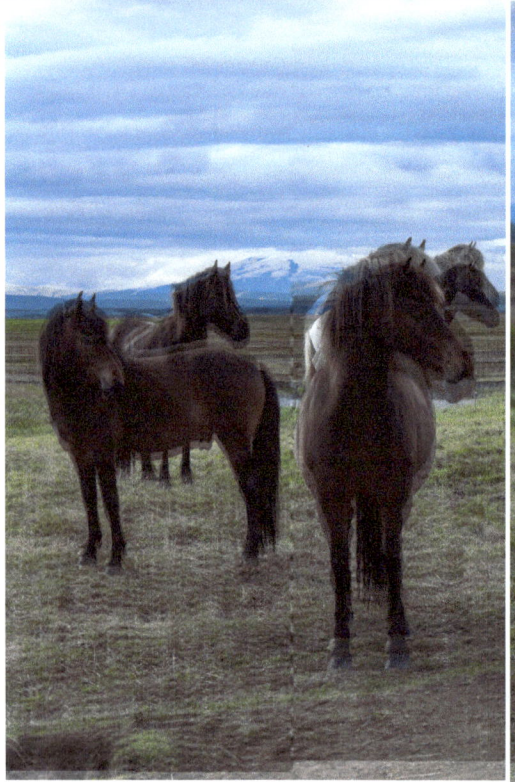
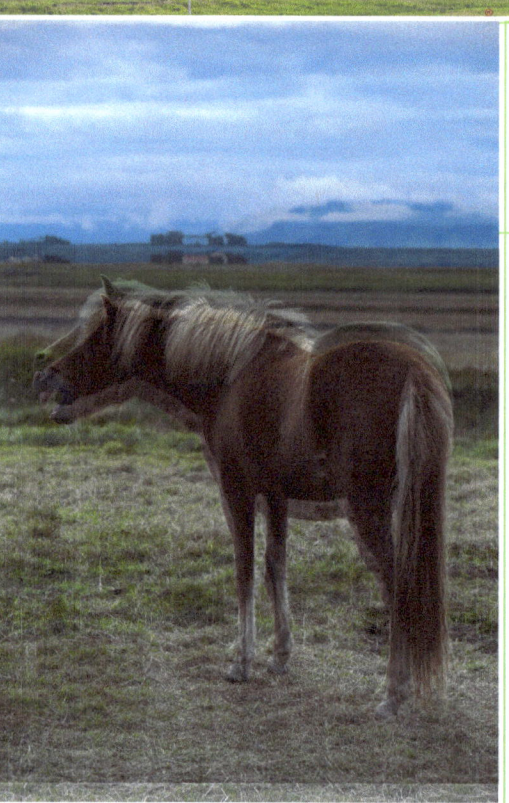

Icelandic Horses, and the Cliffs On The South Shore

Your time is limited; don't waste it living someone else's life. Don't be trapped by dogma, which is living the result of other people's thinking. Don't let the noise of other's opinion drown your own inner voice. And most important, have the courage to follow your heart and intuition; they somehow already know what you truly want to become. Everything else is secondary. -- Steve Jobs

Half the fun of travel is the aesthetic of lostness. — Ray Bradbury

We live in a wonderful world that is full of beauty, charm and adventure, with no end to the adventures if only we seek them. – Jawaharial Nehru

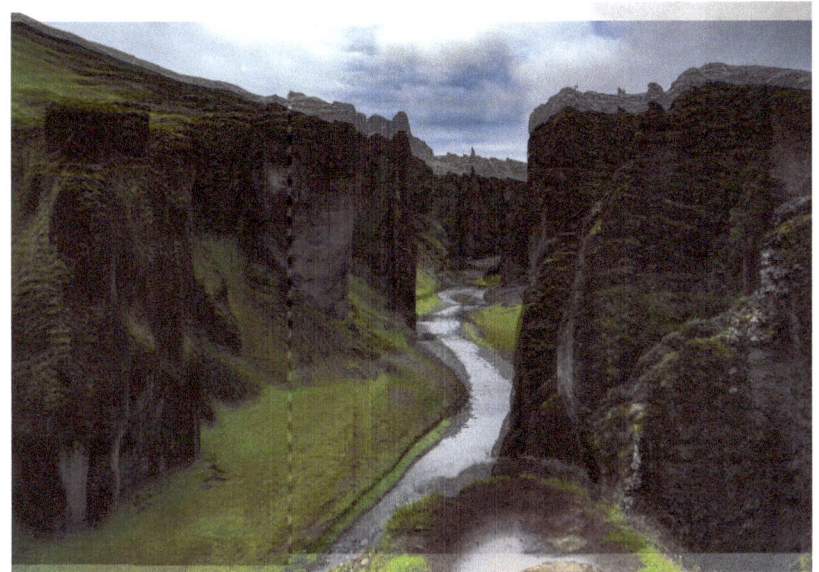

Fjadrargljufur Canyon

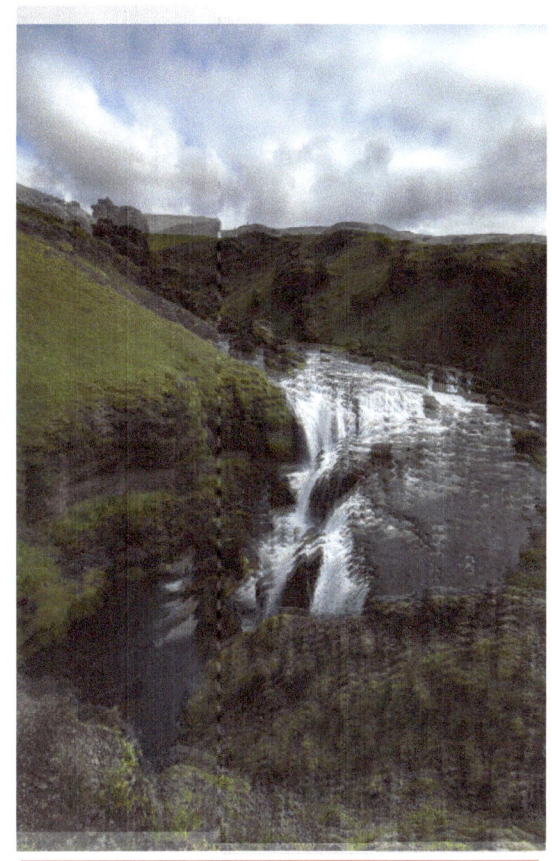

Skogafoss Canyon

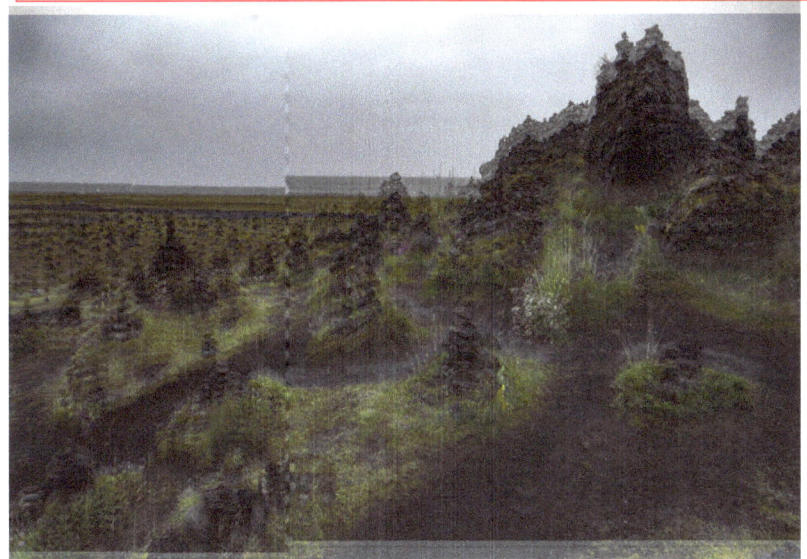

Skaftareldahraun

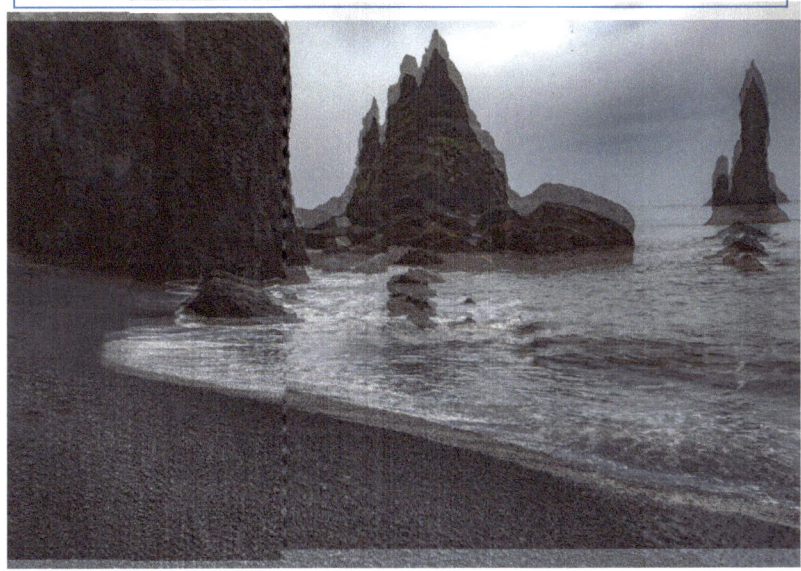

Reynisfjara Beach

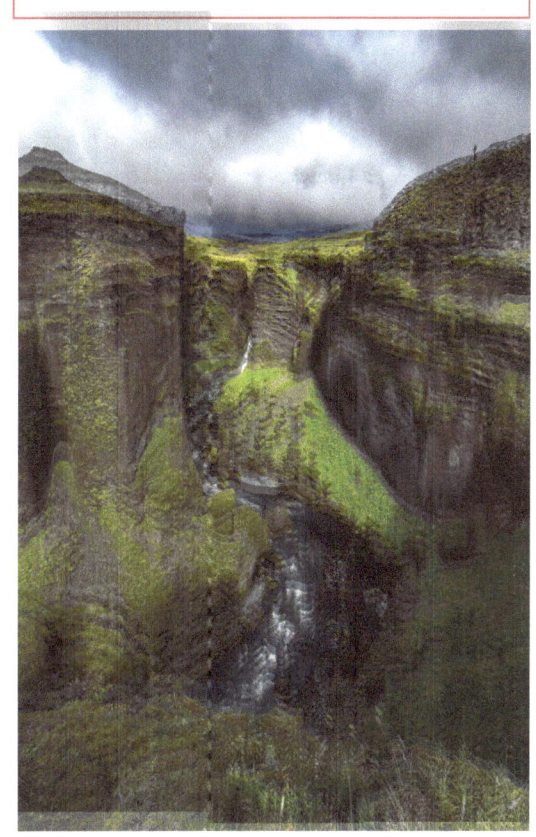

Skogafoss Canyon

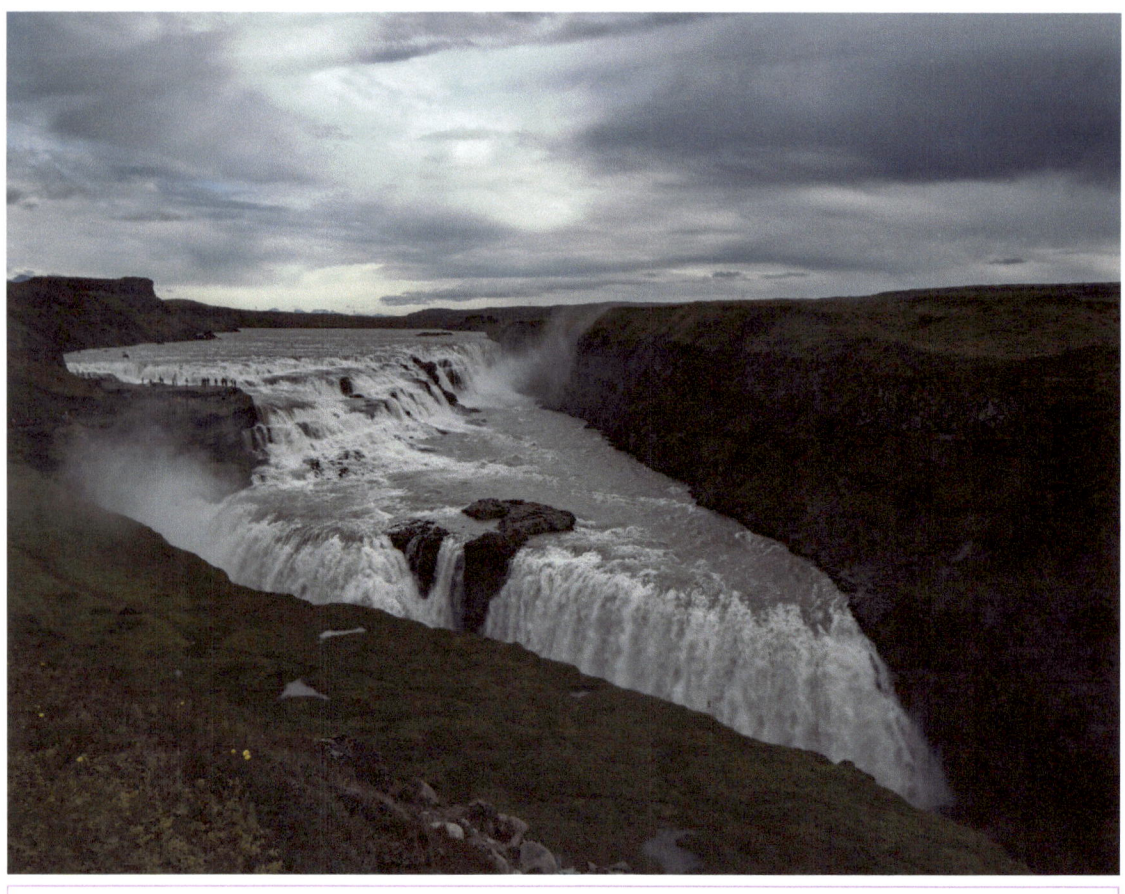

Gullfoss Falls

Twenty years from now you will be more disappointed by the things you didn't do than by the ones you did do. So throw off the bowlines, sail away from the safe harbor. Catch the trade winds in your sails. Explore. Dream. Discover.

Like all great travelers, I have seen more than I remember, and remember more than I have seen. - Benjamin Disraeli

Hope is the only thing stronger than fear. - Suzanne Collins

Because in the end, you won't remember the time you spent working in the office or mowing your lawn. Climb that goddamn mountain. - Jack Kerouac

To travel is to discover that everyone is wrong about other countries. - Aldous Huxley

Blessed are the curious for they will have adventures.

Remember that happiness is a way of travel – not a destination. - Roy M. Goodman

You can shake the sand from your shoes, but it will never leave your soul.

The biggest adventure you can ever take is to live the life of your dreams.

Once in a while it really hits people that they don't have to experience the world in the way they have been told to. - Alan Keightley

Like all great travelers, I have seen more than I remember, and remember more than I have seen. – Benjamin Disraeli

Twenty years from now you will be more disappointed by the things that you didn't do than by the ones you did do. So throw off the bowlines. Sail away from the safe harbor. Catch the trade winds in your sails.

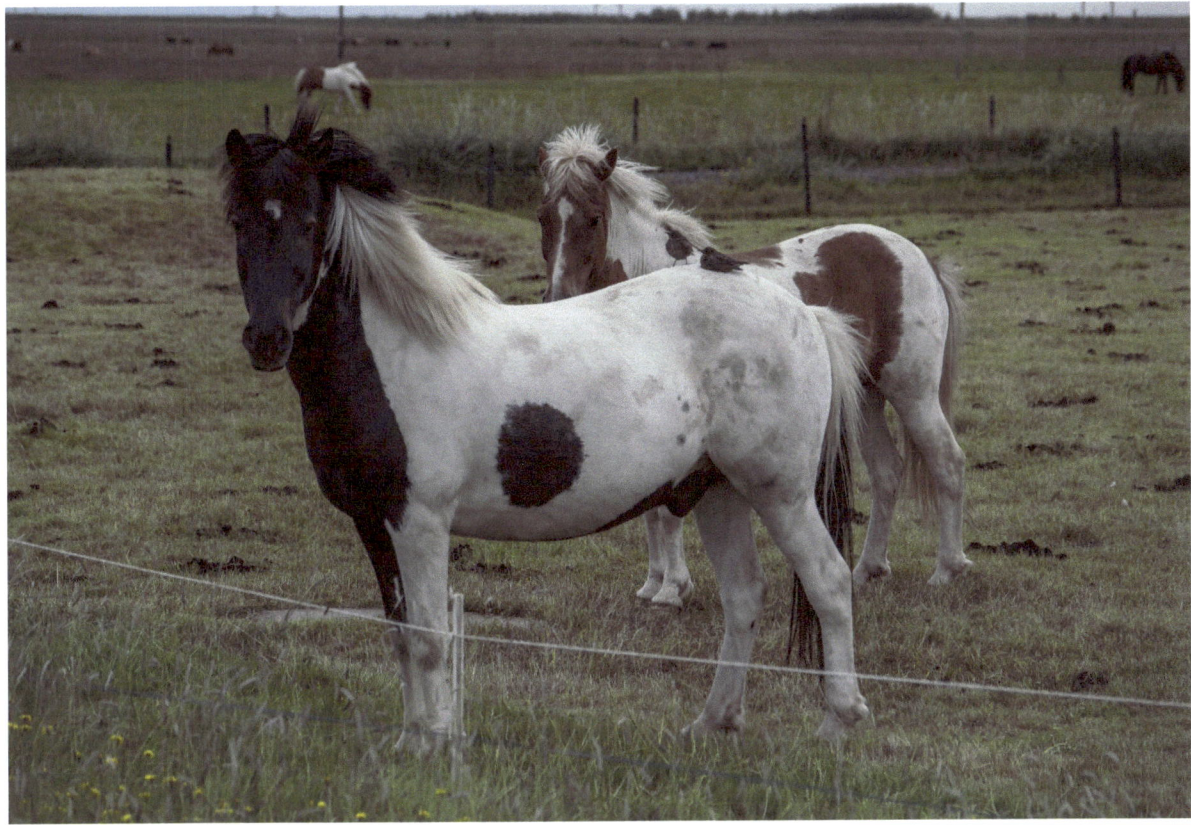

Icelandic Horses

Do not follow where the path may lead. Go instead where there is no path and leave a trail – *Ralph Waldo Emerson*

Focus on the journey, not the destination. Joy is found not in finishing an activity but in doing it.– *Greg Anderson*

Not all those who wander are lost. - R.R. Tolkien

Our happiest moments as tourists always seem to come when we stumble upon one thing while in pursuit of something else. - Lawrence Block

Do not follow where the path may lead. Go instead where there is no path and leave a trail - Ralph Waldo Emerson

Traveling is a brutality. It forces you to trust strangers and to lose sight of all that familiar comforts of home and friends. You are constantly off balance. Nothing is yours except the essential things. air, sleep, dreams, the sea, the sky. all things tending towards the eternal or what we imagine of it. – Cesare Pavese

Every man can transform the world from one of monotony and drabness to one of excitement and adventure. - Irving Wallace

Life is short and the world is wide

We travel, some of us forever, to seek other states, other lives, other souls. - Anaïs Nin

A good traveler has no fixed plans and is not intent on arriving. - Lao Tzu

Life is a journey. Make the best of it.

He who would travel happily must travel light. - Antoine de St. Exupery

I have found out that there ain't no surer way to find out whether you like people or hate them than to travel with them. - Mark Twain

Travel is the only thing you buy that makes you richer.

A journey is best measured in friends, rather than miles. - Tim Cahill

Man cannot discover new oceans unless he has the courage to lose sight of the shore. – Andre Gide

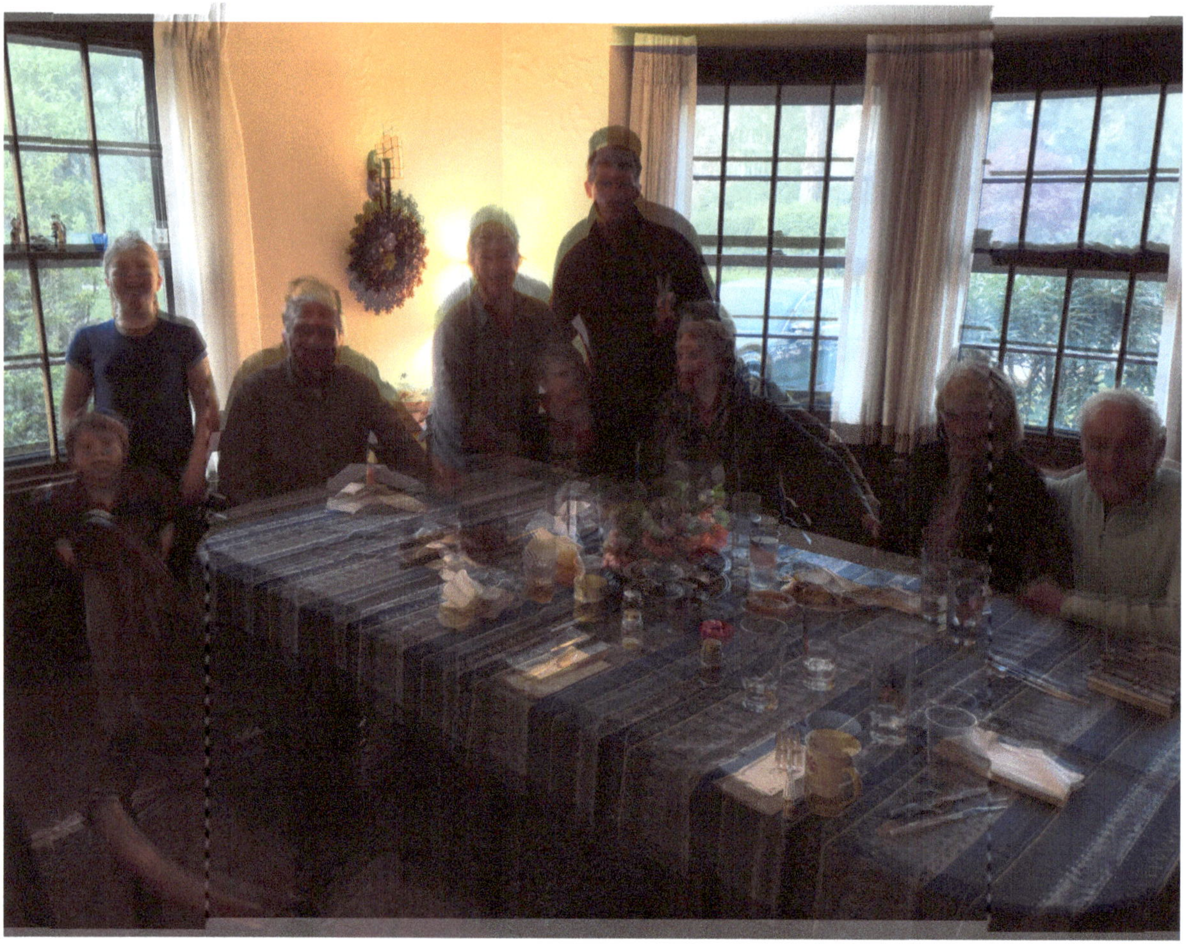

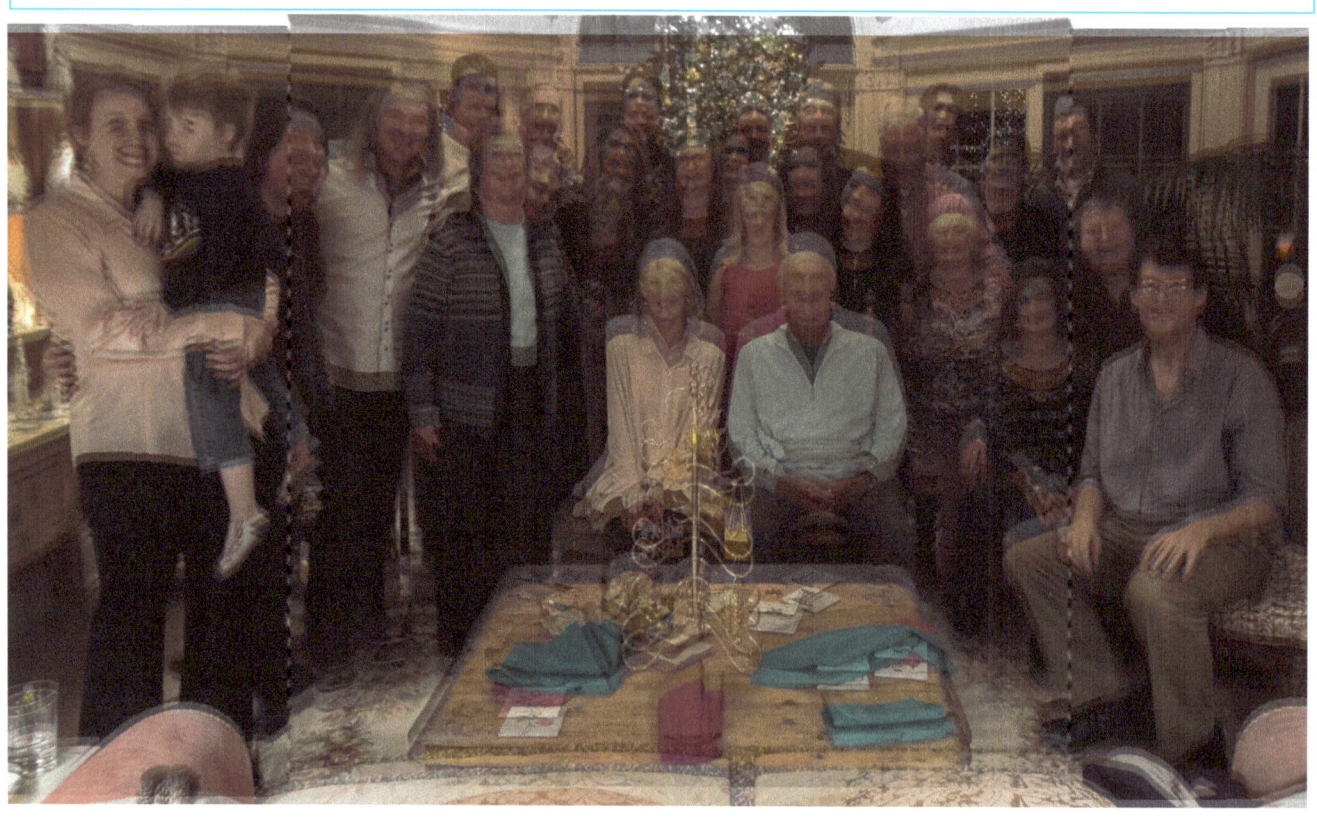

Family Gathering after trip

Extended family at Christmas

Fearlessness

An insatiable curiosity to find the new and exciting in everything, and do without kindness in all actions. Stop looking up peers who are more successful, and be yourself. Do not be on the sidelines, but on the frontlines, and do not watch but invent, for there is no self-loathing and paralysis today, because today is the greatest. Stop the self-hatred and assume control of your destiny and reflection. Blame, control, envy, hate, and resentment are all your enemies. Invent your day and not be consumed by paralysis and fear for mistakes, and choose to say I live free. You create your own demons and the beast and can be free of them. We all experience pain. Pain can be tragic, nonsensical, unjust, undeserved. All of it eventually comes into our lifetime and leaves us with wounds and scars, and our natural instinct is to try and fight it.

Sometimes we can't fix, control, explain, or understand. But this is a place where transformation most easily happens, because there we are in God's hands and not trying to self-manage. Don't get rid of our pain until we've learned what it has to teach us. Use inevitable tragedy, suffering, human loss, betrayal, and death itself not to punish but to bring us closer to God and to our true selves. Our pain needs to become Holy pain. Our wounds become sacred wounds. If we can't find a way to make our wounds into sacred wounds, we will invariably become negative, bitter or depressed. It isn't hard at all to find examples of those who have not dealt well with their pain; our society is filled with them, those who deflect and pass on the pain to others, knowingly or not. Transform the pain and do not deflect or pass on, hold our pain consciously and trustfully, we find ourselves in a very special space. Here we are open to learning and breaking through to a much deeper level of faith. We can find a meaning for human suffering, that God is somehow in it and can also use it for good. Everything can be used for transformation. Forgiveness and peace and transforming love and compassion are healing agents of the process of life. All suffering is redemptive.

Perfectionism is the voice of the oppressor, the enemy of the people. It will keep you cramped and insane your whole life, and it is the main obstacle. The seedlings of stress keep you from the fearlessness, being in the moment and from the fear of keeping the child in you which is the enemy of productivity. The brash cockiness of youth is an extremely precious thing. It's a special kind of fuel that tells you your voice matters. Do not be poisoned by your own sparkplug. Find the untouched innocence and with it a certain lightness. Change is possible in the decay of crippling doubt, and creation happens in change, and leads you to a new height of your potential. Never forget the curiosity into doing something never done before and engage with zest, and say to yourself it is worth trying. Find your flow in the routine, and never plan on being anything less than you are capable of being, or you will probably be unhappy all the days of your life. Experience life rather, and keep your lamps bright and burning, and surrender to the spark of the day. Atonement consists in no more than the abandonment of the self-generated double monster. A dragon thought to be God (superego) and the dragon thought to be Sin (repressed id). But this requires an abandonment of the attachment to ego itself, and that is what is difficult. Tell your story, and satisfy something empty inside creating no death sentence for creativity, and confidence.

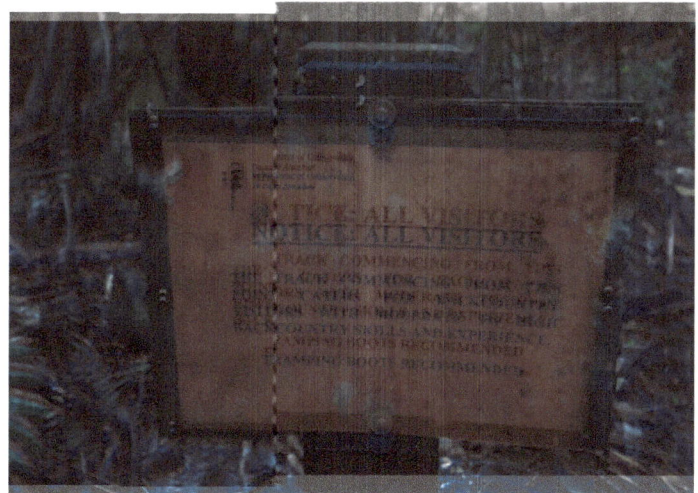

Most important sign on the Journey because now your know you are in the right place

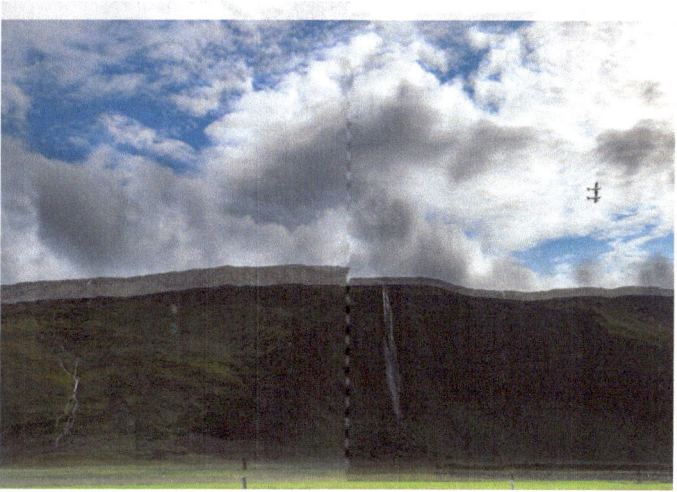

Endless Falls on the South shore of Iceland

Don't become lost and become too scared of your own shadow to dare and try and fail. Never to be too please in your achieving because it is a death sentence for any form of creativity. Find your compass, pick up your sword and enter the cave and do the battle. Find your way through, and find your voice and rediscover your love of your joy. Don't criticize yourself, it hasn't worked for years, approve of yourself and see what happens. Entire new galaxies open up when you grant yourself even the tiniest additional bit of faith, and the elixir of possibility. I believe creativity like human life itself begins in darkness. You can do anything if you don't focus on naked incapacitating jealousy and errors, and find the realms of inspiration where sparks of joy create the infinitely possible. Transition does not happen by being a slave to praise but a way to build the repair your own confidence. When you call yourself out on the crap and destructive habits it can be liberating and profound. What you focus on is your decision and the secret to free will. Be willing to create badly while your ego yelps resistance. Your bad work may be the syntactical breakdown necessary for a shift in your style. Your lousy piece may be pointing you in a new direction. Art needs time to incubate, to sprawl a little, to be ungainly and mis-shapen and finally emerge as itself, and the ego hates this fact. The ego wants instant gratification and the addictive hit of an acknowledged win. Enjoy the joke and find the perfection that exists within all that imperfection. Over time, perfectionism will be defeated. Perfectionism can't survive unless it is fed with the oxygen of indulgence, paranoia and irrationality. Get our of your own way and remember arts purpose which is to make it no matter what life throws are you.

Never forget what some people will do to invalidate the validity of awakening your creative voice, because you are in charge of capturing your dreams. To be fully alive, fully human, and completely awake is to be continually thrown out of the nest. To live fully is to be always in no-man's-land, to experience each moment as completely new and fresh. To live is to be willing to die over and over again. The act of creating has a strange way of manifesting magic into reality. Capture the thoughts and dreams mid-thought and hijack them into creation. Unshackling the shame because vulnerability sounds like truth, and feels like courage. Truth and courage aren't always comfortable, but they're never weakness. Approval can be within and never self doubt always demonstrating value and gratitude to build belief in self. The lizard brain is the reason you're afraid, the reason you don't do all the art you can, the reason you don't ship when you can. The lizard brain is the source of the resistance. Invest in self, create, be noticed, and give yourself authority to lean outward beyond and open doors by leading without being asked to. The grandiose person is never really free; first because he is excessively dependent on admiration from others, and second, because his self-respect is dependent on qualities, functions, and achievements that can suddenly fail. Make a choice to see yourself as a player instead of waiting to be picked and you will be. Stop playing destructive games with perfectionism of being afraid you won't measure up, leading you to do self-sabotaging things like cramming. You have in place an internal belief system in place that you are what you want to be, and say to doubt hey man thank you for sharing. Shake off the cobwebs of shame and doubt and self-hatred. If you have these afflictions, all they're doing is holding you back. Find your life force juice and fail spectacularly, and feel alive because you stretched and something will awaken inside of you.

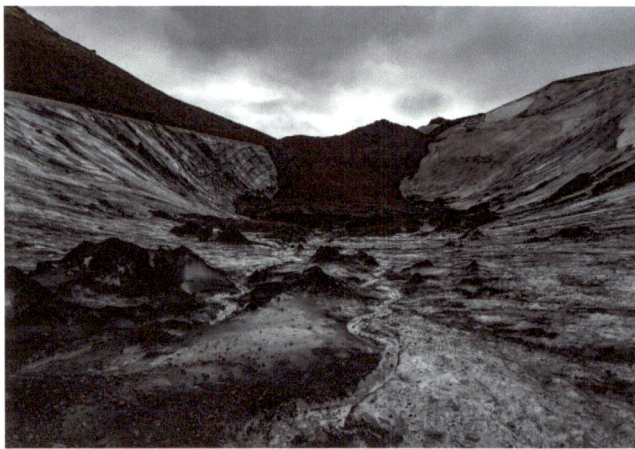

Hike up to Fimmvorduhals Hut

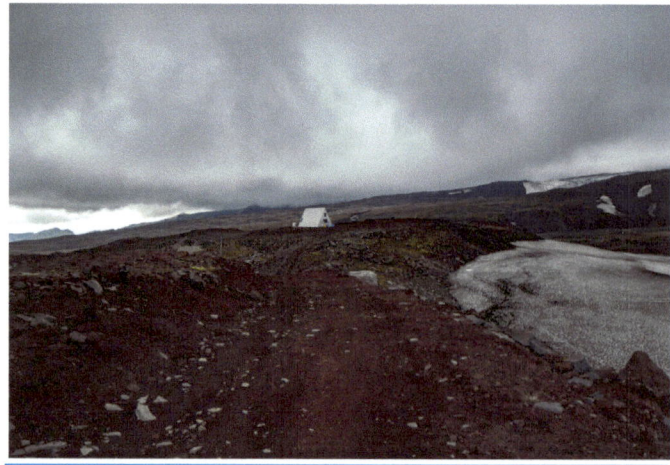

Hike up to Fimmvorduhals Hut

Take those risks and remember it is no the critic who counts but the person who was inside the arena, whose face is marred by dust and sweat and blood; who strives valiantly; who errs, who comes short again and again, because there is no effort without error and shortcoming; but who does actually strive to do the deeds; who knows great enthusiasms, the great devotions; who spends himself in a worthy cause; who at the best knows in the end the triumph of high achievement, and who at the worst, if he fails, at least fails while daring greatly so that his place shall never be with those cold and timid souls who neither know victory nor defeat. Instead of agony, chose to laugh at the absurdity of it all and feel the agency of joy. Your life only stops adding up when you tell yourself that it can't, but in reality, anything is possible and always. Albert Einstein never made any discoveries through the process of rational thinking. You have to be willing to tolerate the discomfort of believing in yourself. Emphasize that anything is possible but you have to change the cellular framework in which you see yourself. Shake off the constant critique of being a failure and allow yourself to succumb to the unthinkable and try but be willing to tolerate the discomfort of believing in yourself. So full of artless jealousy is guilt because it spills itself in fearing to be spilt. No one can make you feel inferior without your consent.

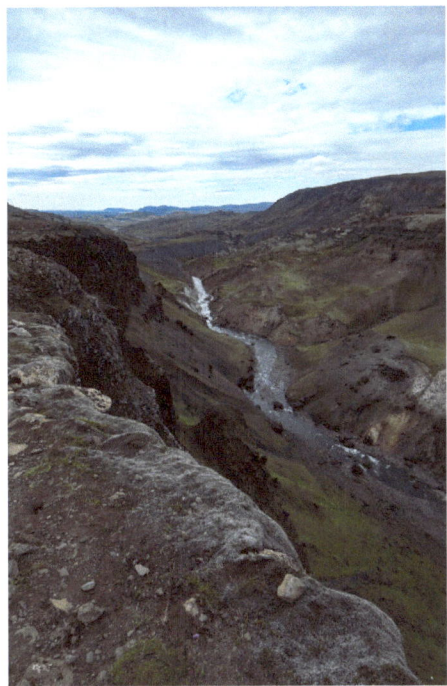

Haifoss Canyon

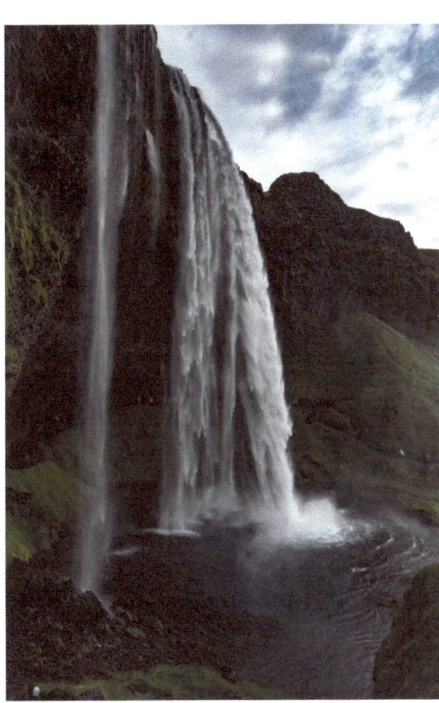

Seljalandsfoss Falls

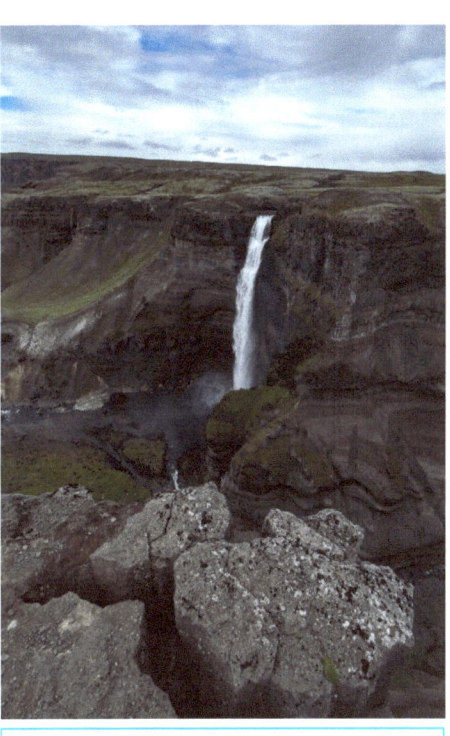

Haifoss Falls

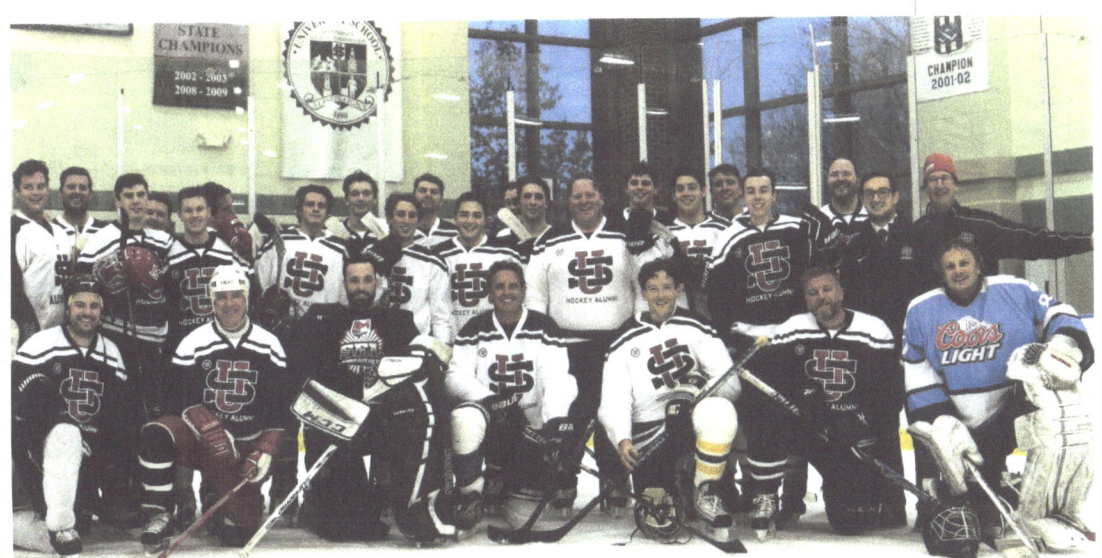

Fun times at the Cleveland Heights Ice Rink trying to play Hockey again after many years of neglect

Gratitude

Ever reached a place where you want to get away from the doldrums of life's precious journey. Maybe you've been tested, tried, and buked by the privileged and their expectations and drama. Maybe your irked by something you recently experienced. You know something is wrong but cant quite put your finger of it, what is it? Perhaps thankfulness has disappeared from your daily routine, and this effective self-care is missing. This feeling of miraculous love and warm feeling of gratitude is always painting in your mind.

Most importantly it remains in those students at any age who soak up the most creativity. What if it were the hardest thing to practice, but you can get the most out of it. Gratitude is when you recognize goodness in everything in your life. It can act as an emotional spackle when we recognize the source of good as outside ourselves. You are the curator of your own moments of joy.

Unfortunately, bitterness, and resentment can creep in. There are people in this world whose sole purpose as a bully is to define themselves by what they hate and they mock things at the expense of others. They gaslight situations and never give others a chance to think independently. At the center of it all it is most important to listen and celebrate what others do in the name of love.

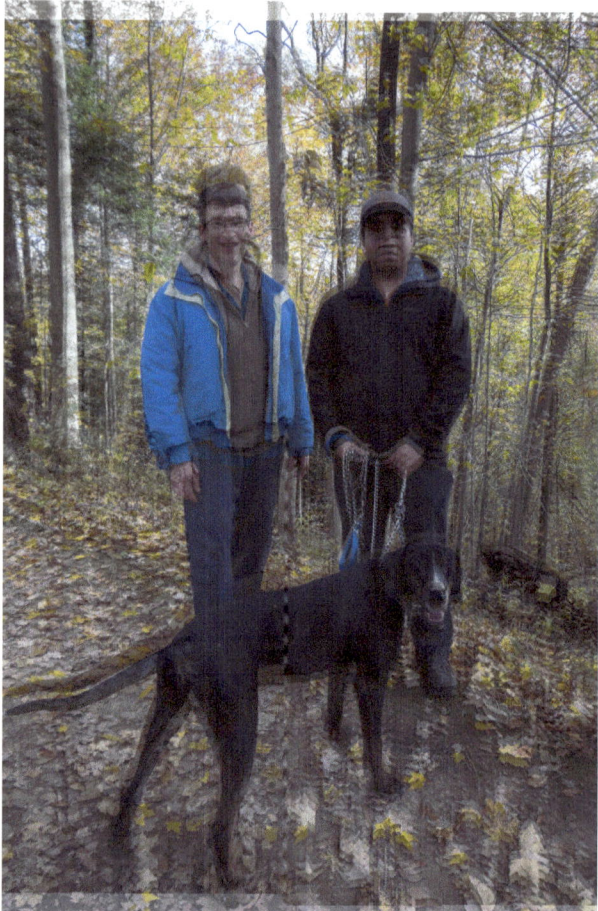

Don Hodell Chilcote, Vinay Pandey, and Awesome Dawson Two-Toned paws Chilcote at North Chagrin Park in Cleveland Ohio

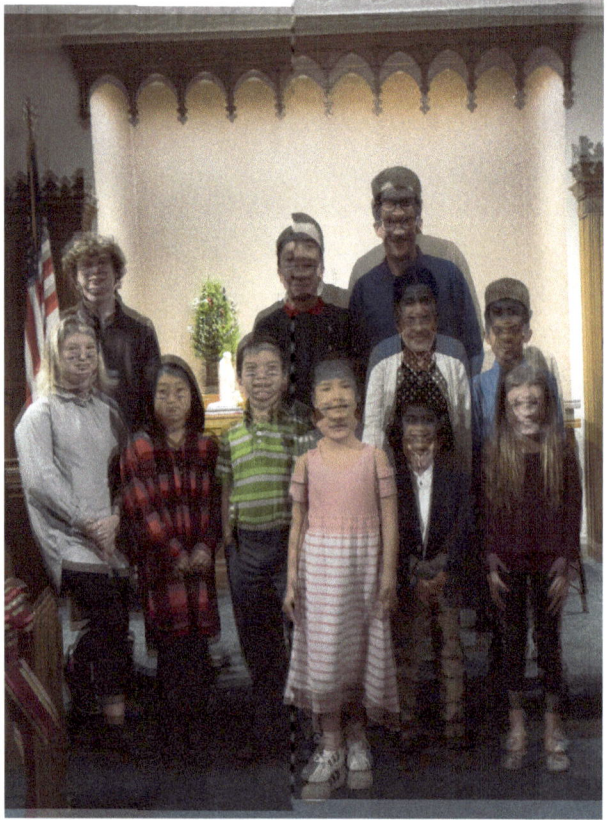

Student Recital at Church Of The Savior

Let gratitude define you. Touch, smell, listen, taste, and capture moments of majesty by generosity, complement, self-control, and unspeakable joy. Find what matters the most and practice the warmth, light, and laughter in your passion, and ability. Celebrate others, celebrate yourself, and your uniqueness as these drive further ambition. Look at the person next to you and practice love, connect with your brother in infectious delight of their joy. Adopt a practice of humor, paradox, and change in daily actions. Be thoughtful and mindful and sensitive about the needs of others.

Hear the cacophony of life, and make harmonious music celebrating the unique traits of the individual. Reveal your true anxieties, fears and hopes and listen with no bitterness or judgment. I believe only in this optimism will you truly grow and be part of something better. Gospel artist, Douglas Miller speaks I'm Troubled, but I'm not distressed, Cast down but I'm not destroyed, I'm tempted and tried, for the Joy of the Lord is my strength. Fluency in mindfulness, thoughtfulness, and unspeakable joy.

From Head To Heart

There is this Gospel song called 'Encourage Yourself,' which guides me often to listen to my heart, and connect through the center. Moment to moment the auditory guidance and persistant inner voice singing seems clear when lifted by intuitions which put you in the right place at the right time. The miracle of synchronicity that results to give you the strength to discover beauty and do good things for this lost world. I always try to cherish old memories in the context of giving and including young hopes. Aligned your giving heart with the ebb and flow of the tides of the seasons of the heart and the revelations of the miracle of connectedness returns us out of nowhere to wonder. Always be a child; always reflect on change, gratefulness, thankfulness; and seeing the good in everything and everybody. Everyday and always let beauty into your soul, and dream a little dream. This book is a celebration of the journeys and the picturesque tales of the soul strengthening, however mind numbing quests.

Only when you connect with nature are you nurtured finding where you belong in this world. You find the value of breathing the pine airs, breathing the ancient volcanic soil, and are restored to safely, and the heart shifts your buoyancy. Abundance and riches in blessings to self and others result when liberated by joy to a state of all encompassing giving. It is in giving that we receive; it is in forgiving that we are forgiven, and it is in dying that we are born into eternal life. Find your treasure wherever the heart is and find your worth in those who hold you up and desire you.

In the end its not about all the times you were bullied or called beautiful; its about the days you felt you were beautiful and the people who make you really feel like you are someone special. In this elevated state never forget the impact you have upon making someone else feel special and wonderful. Do the tried, true, and trusty uniquely and not the damp, stale and musty in auto-pilot. Always invent your path, invent your way, and discover your gift in this world. It is learning that is God's gift to us. Today matters for your choices. Lead others to the pathway of beauty, and show them the magnificent rainbow. Cherish your individuality.

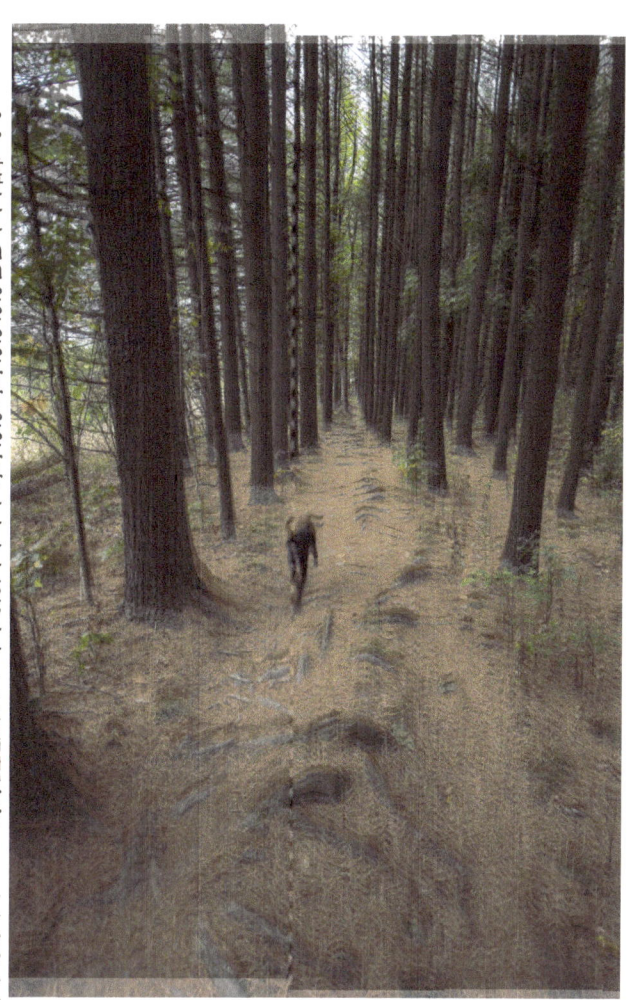

Awesome Dawson Two-Toned Paws in Cuyahoga Valley

Chilcote Family in Cleveland Heights, Ohio

Body And Soul

In this world we all strive for greater humanity, kindness, tolerance and even temperament in the precarious balance of life. A person can learn and grow at any stage of life in their warmth, humor, and deep reverence for newness. The key is a good teacher and a willing heart to see beyond the innocence, and the fluff of existence. In striving for a curious heart that gives, plant the seed of righteousness, virtues and morality build skills to be unique with no guilt. Strive for daily attitude checks and build self esteem by continual encouragement and praise. The highest calling in life is guided by constant inquiry, cherishing of learning, and amazing spontaneity. Open up the reigns and unleash the harness to keep the openness of possibilities remaining humble in the bright horizons. Keep listening to the young as I believe the children are the future, teach them well and let them lead the way. Instill a hard work ethic and liberate an outward reflection of self through unique characteristics that sandwiches inventiveness and inquisitiveness. Learning is God's gift to us. My trail journeys have led me to ask hundreds of questions to the young of today, but not often to the older hiker as they have closed their mind to newness. The tried and true methods set in within an older spirit and often growth can not be obtained. Each Journey has a starting point by no journey remains where it begins.

It is so worth it to accomplish something from struggle than to be handed it without effort. There is a liberation that happens in the journey and a peace in that unselfish quest. There is a renewing of Body and Soul that happens as you fail early, fail often, and fail forward to learn and grow. Thank God for the people who are willing to knock holes in the roof. They are the pacesetters, the barrier breakers, and the miracle producers. They are determined but criticized because they are concerned. Consider it pure joy, my brothers, whenever you face trials of many kinds, remember that the testing of your faith develops perseverance. This perseverance must finish its work so that you may mature and be complete, not lacking anything. (James 1:2-4) If we are unchallenged then we are unchanged, we must get busy living or get busy dying. Gratitude is an elixir to dissolve the hard shell of your ego, be renewed by the journey in the renewing of you mind, body, and spirit. In inventive and inquisitive travels we are planting the seeds of ability, and we are surrendering to the beauty which develops a blissful state. In stepping out of the crowd, we finds glimpses of majesty, and we are surrounded by a lifting cloud that lays aside every weight. Nothing expands possibilities like unleashed thinking. In order for the flower to blossom, you need the right soil of creative thinking and the right seeds of inventiveness.

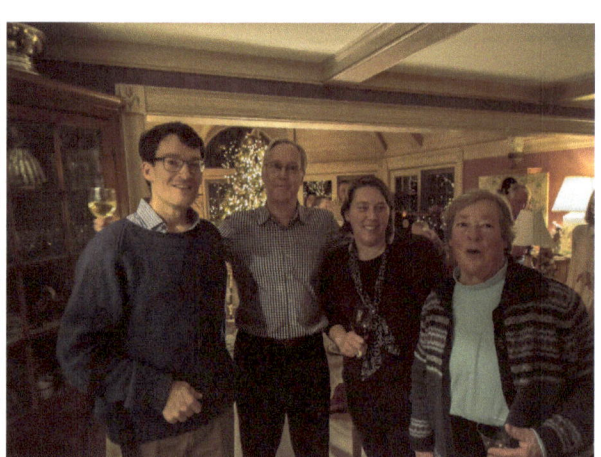

At A Family Gathering in Cleveland Ohio

There is a peace to seek a journey in travels to where there is a Home On The Range where seldom is heard a discouraging word. The old nursery rhyme Row Your Boat is on the most powerful transformational songs in the history of music. Listen and be guided by its continual renewing energies that lie deep and dormant in your soul. The only difference between those who threw in the towel and quit and those who used their energy for crap is the word hope. Hope rebuilds and keeps an under producing thyroid moving and trucking on down the highway. I sing because I'm happy and sing because I'm free, his eye is on the sparrow and I know he watches me. Some people become more satisfied with their positions than their growth and youthful inquisitiveness. We need not be distracted by living monuments of quitters who mark the pathway to the top of the mountain. Finally brothers think on these things: what ever is true, what ever is noble, what ever is right, what ever is pure, whatever is lovely, whatever is admirable. Live, Dream, Breathe, Bless, Give, Journey.

Ending Inspirations

In closing, I have discovered the most important thing in journeys is the uniqueness of the adventure. It is invaluable to me to learn something new, do something not scripted nor planned. I long for the travel on some incredible adventure to find continuing inspiring locations and stories. Most times you have fun, come away with a unique story to tell, and sometimes it just feels like a place you would never go back to. Always guided by the spirit of positivity, and the sense to see it through, and find your soul in some place. You always know that maybe another person has been to this place, but somehow you have something to find within the adventure that turns a corner in your mind. The spirit to have peace with the land has led me back to continue on to find and discovery something distinctive and picturesque.

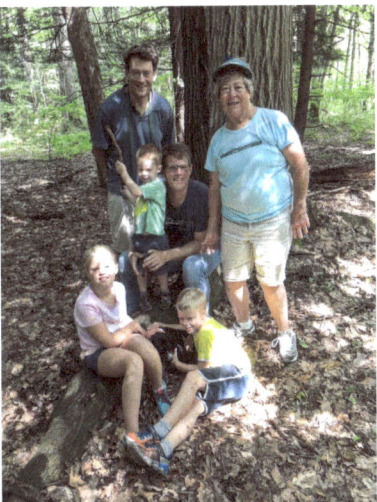

Emily, Johnny, Lee, Nathan, Don, Tuni, at Dobbins Woods

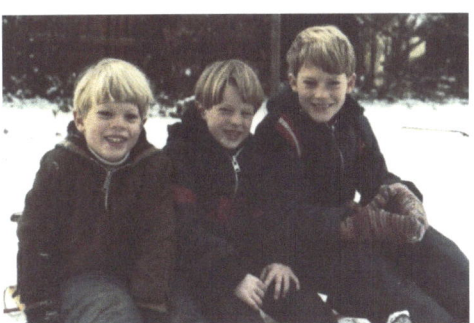

Lee, Mike, Don building snow forts in Cleveland, Ohio

These have been the tales from unquenchable spirit for learning the steps through the garden of discovery over the triumph of the land. The journey has been a challenge, and hopefully leads some of us today to understand the intensity of human spirit to discover the beauty in this world and travel to the ends of the earth. The adventure seems more and more appropriate todays to avoid the instant entertainment and the instant spectacle of life. I have truly invented my own trail and discovered, failed, and toiled. I have tested myself in becoming breakable, but have found and shattered with grace and courage those journeys that strengthen my soul, and of course made art of it all the broken pieces.

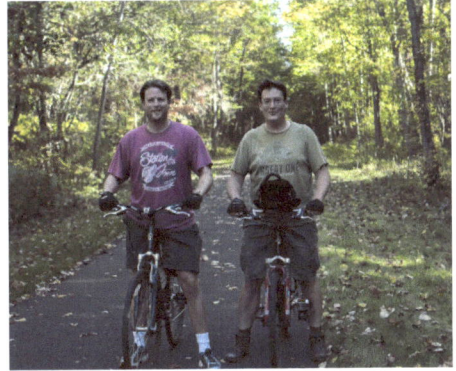

Mike, Don, Biking in Cuyahoga

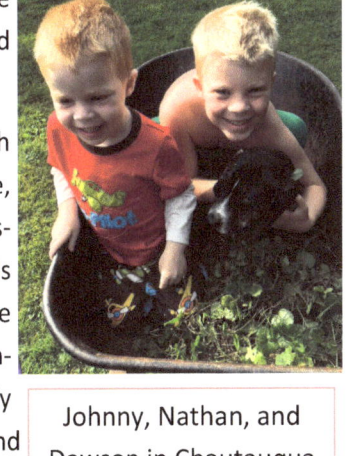

Johnny, Nathan, and Dawson in Chautauqua

The most fun for me is in sharing the journey to those who will listen about the impossible adventure and the story to tell. Every day is truly a gift to make something of it and give back to it each day. Some amazing adventures are yet to unfold and some journeys to far off places like Australia, South Africa, Alaska, Croatia, Finland, Argentina are in on my bucket list and in my dreams as possible destinations. I have no idea whether I'll get there or not as it is not in my hands.

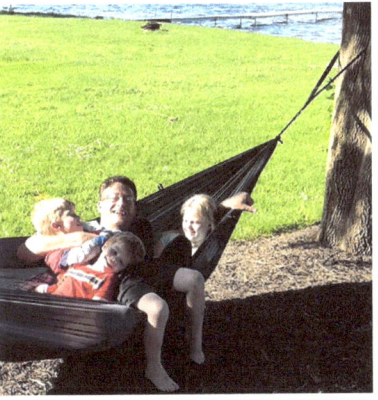

Stuck In a Hammock

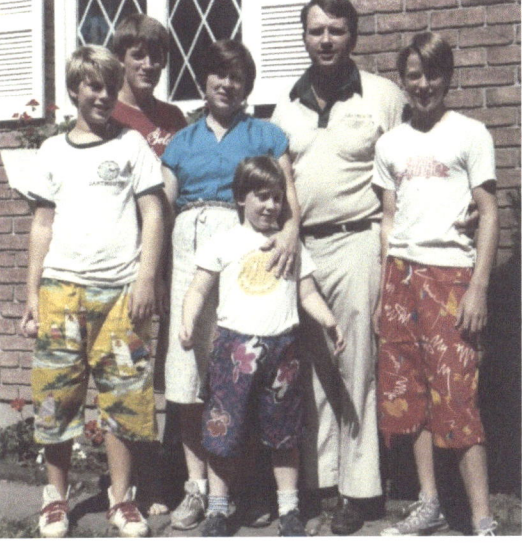

Lee, Don, Tuni, Katherine, Lee, Mike, in Chautauqua, New York

www.ingramcontent.com/pod-product-compliance
Lightning Source LLC
Chambersburg PA
CBHW051924210526

45473CB00006B/2130